Always Think
Canine !

Bob Vetere

Praise for *From Wags to Riches*

"This book doesn't rely on outdated theories about pack leadership with 'alpha dogs' attempting to achieve world domination. *From Wags to Riches* beautifully illustrates what modern behavioral science tells us: the most effective leaders (dog or human) don't force their will on others—they find out what motivates their followers and help them make good choices."

—Victoria Stilwell, world-renowned dog trainer and host of Animal Planet's *It's Me or the Dog*

"Bob Vetere has been a professional champion of a surprisingly resilient sector of our economy: pets. We may scrimp on ourselves, but we'll always find a way to afford the best food for Fido. Now, with *From Wags to Riches*, he explains how business success flows from our understanding—and adopting—some of the same traits animals use to win our devotion. A fun read for alpha CEOs as well as bystanders at the corporate dog run!"

—Michael Schaffer, author of *One Nation Under Dog*

"In this fun read, Robert Vetere brilliantly develops this metaphor between dog-human relationships and solid, collaborative business practices by offering examples from his own fascinating experiences as a successful businessman. Even if you're not a business executive or MBA student, *From Wags to Riches* offers lessons on business (and life) that everyone should know."

—Dr. Alan Beck, director of the Center of the Human Animal Bond, Purdue Veterinary Medicine, Purdue University

"I am a dog lover for over 58 years and have been a business entrepreneur for the past 30 years. How Bob has 'connected the dots' between the similarities of dogs, people, relationships, and business is just phenomenal. Every MBA student, every executive looking to move ahead, and maybe any manger struggling with responsibility, along with anyone who loves dogs and business, needs to read this book. Every chapter is absolutely illuminating and intuitive. At the end of the day, *From Wags to Riches* was like eating comfort food … made me feel warm and cozy. We all can learn a lot from this well-written and entertaining book."

—THOMAS A. COOK, managing director and CEO of American River International, LTD

From *Wags* to *Riches*

*How Dogs Teach Us to Succeed
in Business & Life*

Robert Vetere with Valerie Andrews

BenBella Books, Inc.
Dallas, Texas

BenBella Books, Inc.
10300 N. Central Expressway, Suite #400
Dallas, TX 75231
benbellabooks.com
Send feedback to feedback@benbellabooks.com

Printed in the United States of America
10 9 8 7 6 5 4 3 2 1

Library of Congress Cataloging-in-Publication Data is available
for this title.
ISBN 978-1-936661-10-7

Editing by Erin Kelley
Copyediting by Amy Debra Feldman
Proofreading by Michael Fedison and Nora Reichard
Cover design by Faceout
Text design and composition by Silver Feather Design
Printed by Bang

Distributed by Perseus Distribution
perseusdistribution.com

To place orders through Perseus Distribution:
Tel: 800-343-4499 • Fax: 800-351-5073
E-mail: orderentry@perseusbooks.com

Significant discounts for bulk sales are available. Please contact
Glenn Yeffeth at glenn@benbellabooks.com or (214) 750-3628.

To Brenda, Rob, and Josh
Who bring color, joy, and humor to my life

And to Perseus (2010–2011)
The office dog everyone should have
Gone too soon

Table of Contents

Part III: The Puppy Theory of Management

Part IV: What Dogs Teach Us About Life and Love

Which came first: books on business or books on dogs? I bet if you dug deep enough, you'd find that our interest in dogs and in business goes back almost as far as we do, if for no other reason than for many generations working dogs were part of our "business," as sheepdogs, hunting dogs, sled dogs, guard dogs, and more.

These days, of course, most dogs are "born retired," and animals don't figure much in books on business, with the possible exception of the rodents in the best seller *Who Moved My Cheese? An Amazing Way to Deal with Change in Your Work and in Your Life*. But if you think there aren't some lessons from sharing your life with dogs that can help you in business, then I'd like you to meet my friend Bob Vetere, author of this innovative and entertaining business book.

If the idea seems ridiculous—business advice drawn from dogs?—then you've either never had a dog or never thought much about the great lessons dogs teach us. As a practicing veterinarian, author of bestselling books on pets, and frequent guest expert on *Good Morning America*, I've long been aware of this connection. A resourceful businessman, Bob is an industry leader who is fascinated by the human-animal bond, and well respected among researchers in that field. Over the years he has used stories about his golden retriever to teach the principles of team-work and creativity. His insights will be useful to CEOs and managers, as well as anyone who needs to learn how to "wag their tail" to get ahead in business. There's even a wonderful chapter on the benefits of bringing your dog to work with you.

But you don't have to own a dog to benefit from the lessons in this book. You just have to "think ca-nine"—be open, enthusiastic, and willing to experi-ment. Bob is a funny man, and his sense of humor comes through in stories of CEOs who rely on their doglike wisdom to get some astonishing results.

Bob knows the importance of working in a tight-knit pack, cultivating a doglike empathy for others, sniffing out the competition, and using your canine instincts to tune in to others' moods and emotions. In short, he tells you how to read people as well as a dog can read humans, enabling you to create endur-ing bonds in the workplace.

This smart, fun read will tell much about how to succeed in life and business. Buy it before your competition does. Because as the saying goes, "If you aren't the lead dog, the scenery never changes."

Dr. Marty Becker
"America's Veterinarian"
DrMartyBecker.com

My Dog Is My CEO

Move over, Jack Welch and Warren Buffett. The new role model for business leaders isn't a corporate superstar or one of America's wealthiest tycoons. It's the family dog. What's behind this love affair between top dogs in the corporation and their canine companions? Dogs reflect our social self. They show us how to work in teams and build strong alliances, and they have much to teach us about leadership, loyalty, and trust.

According to an informal poll of CEOs conducted in 2009 by *USA Today*, 67 percent of CEOs surveyed own dogs, compared with 39 percent of the general population. Moreover, these top executives say man's best friend has taught them a good deal about how to succeed in business and in life.

They may be on to something. Dogs are much more than pets that are loved, spoiled, and fretted over. Biologists believe that man's best friend was a kind of genetic pilot for the human race. By keeping us warm, alerting us to danger, helping in the hunt, and cleaning up our scraps, dogs have shown humans how to collaborate.

Canis familiaris appeared on the scene about 16,000 years ago, when people first began to live in groups. Since then, we have built an extraordinary and mutually beneficial partnership with dogs. In the modern era, these animals have helped us herd livestock, deliver mail and medical supplies, and rescue people from fires, earthquakes, and other natural disasters. They've explored outer space, entered the therapy room, and learned to sniff out cancer. Today they are helping us build healthy organizations and refine our concepts of good leadership.

As president of the American Pet Products Association, and a primary supporter of Take Your Dog to Work Day, I've had the opportunity to observe the passionate love affair between dogs and America's CEOs. Not surprisingly, dogs reflect the traits these leaders value most in their coworkers and themselves.

Aggressive bargainers often opt for terriers, famed for their tenacity, while consensus builders tend to prefer herding dogs, known for their ability to move an entire group in the right direction. But it's also true that opposites attract. Tough analytical types often choose goofy, playful dogs like golden retrievers because these animals get them to let down their guard and relax. In these instances, a dog can function as a kind of alternative self, allowing CEOs and managers to express their emotions and engage with others more authentically.

Many examples come to mind of this humanizing effect. John Malone, former chairman, president, and CEO of TCI Communications—once described by former vice president Al Gore as the Darth Vader of the cable industry—appears to soften in the presence of his pugs. Martha Stewart's hard-driven perfectionism has been mitigated by her affection for her chows. Over the years, Ted Turner's beloved black Labrador, Chief, and Ralph Lauren's revered sheepdog, Rugby, seem to have made these iconic leaders more accessible. CEOs talk to their dogs and regularly confide in them because canine companions seem to lessen that feeling of being lonely at the top. In addition, they bring these hard-nosed leaders back to a state of childhood innocence. As the fiercely competitive head of Chrysler, Lee Iacocca, reportedly said, "There are times when even the best manager is like the little boy with the big dog waiting to see where the dog wants to go so he can take him there."

According to the *USA Today* poll, 77 percent of CEOs who own a dog judge the character of their friends and business associates based on how they treat their animals. "I would love to have the intuition my rottweiler (Chester) has," Dave Young, former CEO of Verlo Mattress Factory Stores in Fort Atkinson, Wisconsin, says in the *USA Today* article. He "makes judgments about people that turn out to be amazingly accurate." Honesty and integrity are the values that Ben Golub, former CEO of Plaxo, an online networking company in Mountain View, California, associates with dogs. "Never work with someone whose dog isn't overtly happy to see them when they get home, or vice versa," he told the newspaper.

Hollywood mogul Barry Diller and fashion designer Diane von Furstenberg are known to take their dogs to meetings to put their business associates at ease, while chef Rachael Ray and Ty Pennington, the contractor and host of *Extreme Makeover*, use their dogs to boost the level of enthusiasm in their organizations.

The good news is that you don't have to own a dog to get these benefits.

In this book, you'll learn how to become a more effective leader by tapping into the instinctive part of the brain we share with dogs. While we tend to overestimate dogs' capacity for logic, these animals do have a superior emotional intelligence. Almost any mutt can teach us a good deal about patience and the ability to listen noncritically to others. They also have an uncanny way of assessing people's motives by reading their body language. All dogs carefully guard their physical resources. Following their example means taking careful stock of our assets, sniffing out new opportunities, and looking out for the good of the pack. We would do well to emulate other canine qualities, too. Service breeds, like German shepherds and Labradors, exhibit high levels of stamina and perseverance and are bred to think creatively when facing unexpected challenges.

Finally, dogs act as our "chief exuberance officers," reminding us that work and play can (and should!) feel like the same thing.

For the past thirty-five years, I've drawn on canine behavior to teach management seminars and foster innovation and creativity. In this book, I'll show how dozens of business leaders employ the principles I describe to enhance productivity and boost their bottom line.

Part one shows how much we have to gain by learning to read our coworkers as well as our dogs read us. Dogs specialize in nonverbal communication to an extent that seems almost telepathic. British scientist Rupert Sheldrake has demonstrated that dogs tune into their masters as if they were sending out a homing beacon. Similarly, neuropsychologist Stanley Coren wrote in *Modern Dog* magazine that dogs have an uncanny ability to read our gestures and recognize our moods. When you encourage your staff to respond to each other with the same fidelity and level of attention that dogs focus on their human partners, you'll end up with a tight-knit team known for their superb communication, and your staff will take more joy in their work.

This first section of the book also shatters the myth of the alpha dog and explains why good management all comes down to sharing responsibility and winning the friendship and loyalty of the group. In fact, dogs bred and raised together don't fight for dominance; instead, members of the pack change roles depending on the task at hand. In short, man's best friend isn't into power trips.

Interestingly, Generations X and Y prefer to work in packs, sharing roles and responsibilities. Enlightened managers need to take these new work styles into account, move away from "command and control," and embrace a canine model of collaboration and teamwork.

Next, my coauthor and I have developed the "What Breed Are You?" test to help you identify your leadership style. The test will tell you what well-known entrepreneurs have in common with bloodhounds, what legacy CEOs have in common with rottweilers, and what motivational leaders have in common with golden retrievers. It will also help you identify your strengths and weaknesses, and see how you are perceived by the rest of the pack.

Part two shows how a relaxed workplace fosters innovation and creativity. Dogs learn best when an activity feels like play; they will keep at a task for hours, as long as it's fun and challenges their inventiveness. But the moment it becomes drudgery, they disengage. Manage your staff in the same way: do whatever it takes to keep them stimulated and to keep the job feeling fresh. The moment work becomes routine, find a way to change the focus.

I first realized that dogs have a good deal to teach us about the link between play and innovation when I served as a director at First Brands in the 1980s. Our research and design group wasn't coming up with new product ideas fast enough, so I tried something different: I told stories about my retriever, Samson, to show my staff how to problem-solve. To kick off the meeting, I recounted the endless strategies he used to tunnel underneath the backyard fence or to retrieve a ball that had gotten stuck beneath a neighbor's van. Samson was a non-threatening role model: he distracted everyone from their usual competition and self-consciousness and helped us to engage in the kind of "serious play" that has real payoffs.

Innovation is what keeps any company afloat. You're in deep trouble when your new people are afraid to take risks, and when the pressure to come up with a new product is so intense even your veteran team members start freezing up. The homework assignment for this group was to go to the dog park and watch how dogs moved from one activity to the next, unhampered by those two great human inventions: anxiety and fear of embarrassment.

When I moved on and became vice president of Oil-Dri Corporation of America, a major producer of agricultural and pet products, I started to run my area of the company like a dog pack and developed what I now call "The Puppy Theory of Management."

Rule number one is to reward in real time. Don't wait for the annual review to recognize an employee contribution or pat somebody on the back. People need to know what they're doing right or wrong— and they need to know immediately. I'm not talking about old-fashioned behaviorism, the notion that you can guarantee a good performance by offering a treat or eliminate bad habits by taking that reward away. I'm talking about giving your people ongoing feedback and building the kind of relationship that makes them eager to take on new challenges.

You'll also get results if you follow four other dog-training principles: correct early, stay on message, lead by example, and encourage intelligent disobedience. The first three principles are considered "best practices" by many human resource experts, but the last one may be less familiar. A good guide dog is taught to disobey his handler if, by doing so, he can save someone from harm. Effective CEOs and managers foster independent thinking instead of feeling threatened by it, allowing their employees to ignore the rules when doing so will serve a higher good.

Bad CEOs tend to behave less like guide dogs and more like lone wolves. A lone wolf, by definition, is an outcast, a creature that's cut off from its larger kinship group. The animal's behavior is dangerous or unpredictable. Rogue CEOs are similar, and their predatory behavior has seriously damaged the American business climate in recent years. Leaders like this tend to ignore the well-being of the pack, and when they fail, they fail spectacularly, taking entire companies and entire industries down with them.

Another lesson we can take from the canine world: dogs don't tolerate bad leaders. If a dog falters and falls down on the job, he is immediately replaced by another member of the pack. If we followed the canine example, we'd depose incompetent leaders long before they had a chance to wreck a firm. Instead, we humans tend to rationalize bad behavior and make excuses for an incompetent or self-serving boss.

This book tells you what do when a CEO or manager has gone off track. It also offers tips for handling bad hires and dealing with "bad dog" behavior in your direct reports. Animal trainers often say: don't blame the dog. Instead look at the messages he's getting and address the communication problem. I'll explore when to retrain problem employees or to place them in a job that is a better fit, and when their "bad behavior" is so damaging to others that you have to let them go.

Part three of this book considers the canine model of transparency. Back in the fourth century BC, the Greek philosopher Diogenes suggested that we emulate the dog because this animal is unfailingly honest and always does his business out in the open. Diogenes called himself a Cynic—the original meaning of that word was not "one who has little faith in his fellow man" but "one who is doglike and direct." A Cynic was simply a person who believed in our modern notion of transparency, who behaved in a forthright manner and had no hidden agendas. We've seen what happens when leaders ignore this canine standard of behavior. Who can forget the backroom deals at places like Enron and WorldCom?

Part four focuses on how dogs can teach us to build successful relationships and find joy in our daily lives. Over the past ten years, I've had wonderful jobs that required long hours and gave me lots of frequent flyer miles. During this time, I can honestly say that my three retrievers kept my family grounded, and kept our lives in balance. My wife, our two sons, and I looked forward to our weekend—time together, playing with our dogs. Our retrievers, first Samson, then Wharf, and now Dakota, were an important bridge, helping me to transition from high-powered meetings back to family life. An afternoon with Dakota still remains one of our primary ways to relax and reconnect.

My organization has recently joined forces with the Purdue University School of Veterinary Medicine to create a center that explores the human-animal bond. It is headed by Dr. Alan Beck, who has already done some groundbreaking research, showing how dogs help us to nurture one another and give back to our communities. Man's best friend has a good deal to teach us about generosity: how to be more open-hearted with family, friends, and others in our community. I've found that as I develop my canine ability to engage and respond to others, I have stronger ties with my children, spouse, friends, and neighbors. Studying dogs has enabled me to find greater success and happiness, not just in the corner office, but in every corner of my life. After reading this book, I hope you'll experience the same benefits.

Robert Vetere
South Windsor and Greenwich, Connecticut
December 2011

PART I
A Guide to Dogged Leadership

"All knowledge, the totality of all questions and all answers, is contained in the dog."
—Franz Kafka

Chapter 1

The Canine Connection

W hile it's folly to expect your dog to read a spreadsheet, he's a veritable Einstein when it comes to the nuances of relationships.

There's a courting dance that dogs are known for—one that makes them better at winning friends and influencing people than the eponymous Dale Carnegie. As the humorist Jerome K. Jerome once said, "Dogs never talk about themselves, but listen to you while you talk about yourself, and keep up the appearance of being interested in the conversation."

It's not an act; dogs do indeed pay rapt attention to every human word and gesture. In fact, they've been studying us for at least 16,000 years: first to see if we'd share our hearth and scraps, then to insinuate their way into our hunting parties. As they helped us kill large mammals, dogs got to share in the spoils, and in the process, they learned to decipher our subtle body language and facial cues. New research indicates that dogs can read our responses better than any other species. Daniel Mills, a professor of veterinary behavior medicine at the University of Lincoln, England, found that dogs have noticed that humans don't reveal their emotions symmetrically—the right side of the human face tends to be more expressive than the left side. So far, according to Mills, no other animal has figured this out. When dogs look at each other, they don't discriminate between the left and right side of the face; they developed this behavior specifically for interacting with us.

As every dog lover knows, dogs can tell whether we're happy, sad, calm, or angry, and will often offer comfort. When a stranger approaches, they can, to an amazing degree, decipher the person's intentions and discriminate between friend and foe.

In my experience, the best CEOs and managers, like dogs, have a high degree of emotional intelligence. They know how to read the moods of their clients and staff and make a constant effort to engage others. When I was a young engineer at Union Carbide, I was put in charge of a department, supervising people twenty years my senior. I had plenty of technical knowledge, but I was an inexperienced leader. The first few weeks I tried to be invisible, hoping no one would catch on, and the workers did their best to ignore me. When I got home each night, I felt like the loneliest person in the world. But as soon as I took my Irish setter, Shannon, to the park, my spirits lifted. I watched her sidle up to everybody we met along the jogging path, bow to them and plead to be petted, and then nuzzle up and win them over one by one. Then it finally dawned on me: to succeed as a manager, I had to take a cue from my furry friend, learn to "wag my tail at others," get to know my staff.

Lead with Your Heart, Not Just Your Head

If you stop and think about it, Rover doesn't miss a trick: he zeroes in on your body language and your tone of voice, and through some kind of canine mind-meld, knows exactly what you're feeling every minute. And, of course, he regards you as if you're the most important person in the world.

Leadership is about connecting with people on this level. You've got to "dog your people" to really understand them, and know what motivates them and makes them tick. Trouble ensues when managers become too distant or too isolated and their staff members often feel unheard and unsupported. There's one thing I can guarantee: there will be a corresponding drop in productivity every time you check your feelings and your personality at the door.

Employees want the same basic contract we have with dogs, one that is based on mutual enthusiasm, and a code of service, loyalty, and trust. This relationship is perhaps the most effective and sophisticated nature has produced. If you're the top dog, and you're not paying close attention to your staff, you're only half a leader. And your employees will constantly be feeling like lost pups.

To establish yourself as the true leader of the pack, create an informal space—very much like a dog run—where you get to know your colleagues and coworkers. Of course, that's the rationale behind most corporate retreats. But instead of having one lavish blowout every year, hold several mini-sessions—such as a two-hour lunch meeting in each department—until you've covered all the bases, because it's easier to build intimacy and trust in small groups.

In these sessions, I invoke the special relationship we have with dogs and encourage people to keenly observe their teammates. "Dogs know us better than we know ourselves," I tell them. "They process every gesture and facial tic and know how to read the tenor of our voices. They decipher our needs and wishes, our intentions and our motivations in the same canny way they learned to read a trail, or track a scent. What if we were as observant of each other? How would this change the way we feel about our colleagues? And how would this change the way we work?"

According to a study by Dr. Albert Mehrabian at the University of California, Los Angeles, people respond 7 percent of the time to the words you're saying, 38 percent of the time to your tone of voice, and 55 percent of the time to your facial expressions, body position, hand gestures, and other forms of physical communication. That means the bulk of your communication is physical, not aural.

Since a salesperson has only seconds to convey the company's product or message, many successful transactions depend on his ability to decipher a potential customer's feelings, facial expressions, and subtle body cues. To handle complex situations, a customer service representative also needs to be adept at reading and responding to nonverbal clues.

Finally, managers need to align their body language with their words; otherwise, employees will pick up on any dissonance or internal conflict and be confused.

My friend Dr. Marty Becker, the resident veterinarian on *Good Morning America*, says that it's impossible to mislead a dog. "I dare you to get out of the chair and try to fake your dog out," he once challenged me. "Go ahead. Make a gesture that means the opposite of what you intend."

When it was time for Wharf's walk, I sat down in a chair and opened *The New York Times*, as if I had no intention of taking him to the park. I must have glanced briefly toward the door, however, because Wharf was there in a flash with his leash in his mouth. When I told Becker about this, he started laughing.

"Your dog knows which gesture means walk, treat, or play ball," he said, "even if you've got your nose in the newspaper and you're sitting down. He knows you better and reads your cues better than another human could."

Reading your coworkers might not be a snap, but there are a few basic rules. When you make a suggestion about a project, or tell someone how to improve their performance, you need to watch that person's face and ask, "Did they really like what I just said?"

Your marketing director may be nodding affirmatively, but her body is saying no to your idea if she's pursing her lips, rubbing her neck, or clenching her jaw. We have no control over these displays of discomfort or dissent. The limbic brain just answers for us, doing what it has done for thousands of years.

Dogs have their own system of universal signals: if they jump forward and growl, that's a sign of raw aggression. If they lower their heads, crouch, and wag their tails, it's an invitation to friendship. We're constantly giving out these kinds of clues as well.

I give my staff a few simple guidelines: make eye contact as much as possible to show your openness and receptivity. Observe the body language of others. Are your team members leaning toward you, showing an eagerness to listen, or are they slumped in their chairs? If their hands are clenched or their arms are folded tightly in front of their chests, then you've lost them. Their body language is saying, "I'm bored," "I'm angry," or, "I disagree with you."

Without realizing it, we tend to mirror other people's breathing rates, so if a colleague is agitated, others will often adopt a similar shallow breathing pattern. This is how negative emotions can infect an entire room. When a discussion gets tense, I suggest everyone take a deep breath and then take a momentary break from the topic on the table.

Movement is also a great way to calm the body. If someone has gone on the defensive, sometimes I'll ask my staff to leave the conference room and join me on a walk. As we synchronize our pace, we also synchronize our breathing and our heart rates, until we experience what psychologists call "entrainment"—the ability to tune into your companions' moods. After this, we can sit back down and tackle any problem more effectively.

Learn to Read Your Employees' Moods

People with a canine ability to read their coworkers' moods are generally the emotional leaders of a company. Folks turn to them when the work isn't going smoothly, they have a personal problem, or their job is no longer a "good fit." These people fill an important role day-to-day because they know when people are happy and when they feel overburdened, under-appreciated, or too stressed to do their best work.

Such leaders also play an important role in economic downturns, for they instinctively know how to listen and to boost employee morale. "We learned how significant these doglike managers are when the economy slumped in [the] early 1980s," management consultant Elizabeth Kirkhart, cofounder of Moving Boundaries in Gresham, Oregon, said in an interview. "Air traffic controllers went on strike and President Reagan fired more than 11,000 of them across the nation." Only a core group remained, and Kirkhart was called in to help rebuild the organization. One regional manager emerged as the natural leader because he had a doglike ability simply to listen and be empathetic.

Kirkhart, who now trains leaders around the world, said the ability to understand and relate to many types of personalities is crucial. "A lot of our coaching focuses on helping managers interact with people," she said, adding that she finds the documentary *The September Issue* to be the "perfect training film."

The September Issue shows the inside workings of *Vogue*, a magazine that sets the pace for the fashion industry. In the documentary, editor Anna Wintour comes across as a cerebral and isolated boss. She has an unerring eye for trends, but she relies on the magazine's creative director, Grace Coddington, to keep things running smoothly on a daily basis.

Coddington bounds around the office like a golden retriever, making sure her colleagues feel appreciated. She's wonderfully spontaneous and funny. She even lures the documentary filmmaker—a middle-aged guy with a slight paunch—into a photo shoot, pairing him with a thin model in a party dress. Later, when the art director starts to retouch that paunch, Coddington says, "No way. This guy is a real person!" Her greatest gift is her doglike sense of playfulness and acceptance: she doesn't take herself, or the world of haute couture, so seriously that work becomes routine.

Try a Canine Walkabout

So many managers complain, "I don't find out what's wrong in time to fix it because people don't tell me. They're afraid to come into my office and voice their insecurities and doubts."

CEOs often *assume* that things are running smoothly, but the reality is that they're actually out of the information loop because few people are willing to take a risk and give them honest or constructive feedback. It's a truism that the higher up the line you go, the less likely you are to get useful feedback. And the problem is even worse for women and minorities. So how do you find out what's really going on?

One option is to hire a chief operating officer or vice president who has canine instincts and is skilled at listening to people's problems and at soliciting opinions that employees might hesitate to share with you directly. This job is more than just a "listening post"—it's about shaping company morale. The person who holds this position has to ensure that people's needs are met on a day-to-day basis, and that the organization has both a consistent vision and a way of rewarding employee contributions at every level.

My advice for the person who fills this role: don't just sit there in the corner office, handing out instructions. Instead, do what any self-respecting dog does: wander around for the purpose of building new alliances.

My dog, left to his own devices, would jump the fence at night, cross rivers and streams, and brave the highway just to be near other dogs. If you could follow him, you'd begin to understand his special genius. He's gathering information, building networks, and extending his sphere of influence.

A good leader does this on a regular basis. When I started at Union Carbide, I took my dog to the office right before the shifts changed. As people stopped work, they were eager to engage with my dog and were often willing to chat with me about what was going on at every level of the company. I wondered how I could get the same response when I was on my own. Over time, I learned how to approach people—including some employees I'd never met—and talk to them about their hopes and dreams, and their roles in the company.

Recently I discovered a new variation on that theme: Omar Hamoui, former CEO of AdMob, a mobile advertising company, would not only roam the halls, but also move his desk to different parts of the building. "My whole office construct is nomadic," he told *The New York Times*. "About every six weeks or so I move to another part of the company that I haven't heard a lot about lately, or where I don't know the people. I just pick up my computer and go sit somewhere else."

Whether you move your office or just yourself, you'll soon discover the benefits of this approach. Within a few minutes of seeing you, staffers are likely to share their excitement about a new product and to air their concerns if things aren't going well. All you have to do is activate your doglike curiosity, widen your territory, and start to "sniff around."

Cultivate a Doglike Openness and Honesty

A dog has such a fine-tuned moral sense that he can't hide the fact that he's done something wrong. Today's managers not only have to be good listeners and facilitators—they also need to be more candid about their own gaffes. You might not believe it, but there are advantages to being this up front with everyone. Self-revelation may seem uncomfortable at first, but it allows you to set the stage for a real dialogue where managers and workers can be open with each other and learn from their mistakes.

When I was a young manager at Union Carbide, I had to make some cuts in staff and I did so arbitrarily. Later, I realized that I'd eliminated the two key people in my department: one was the innovator; the other was the emotional leader. When I realized my error, I went to the vice president and begged for the money to rehire them. Fortunately, he agreed. From that point on, I made sure I knew who was performing a key task and which team members were indispensable. I tell that story to my managers to illustrate how easy it is to foul up, and to indicate that the best policy is to admit when you've messed up.

When you model this kind of openness and transparency, you make it easier for people to come to you when a project is about to run off track. And then you can act *before* the situation turns into a full-blown crisis.

I believe you should make it a practice to tell people what's going wrong at the highest level of the organization, too. It may be hard to say, "Hey, look. We've got a problem with the board," or, "Someone in accounting made a major error and we have less money than we thought." But if you don't share your revelations, they won't surprise you with theirs. Remember, the top dog has to be the one to set the tone.

This kind of honesty can help you win over your customers as well. When I was vice president of Oil-Dri ten years ago, the company was in deep trouble. Gas prices were going through the roof, making it much more expensive to ship our products, and that meant we had to raise our prices. The CEO, Dan Jaffee, gathered the senior staff and asked, "How are we going to fix this?" It was a bad situation and there was no way we could sugarcoat it, so we decided to be straight with our customers. We created an ad campaign that said, "You've already been hit with rising gas costs at the pump. We know this is a second punch. But if you stand with us we'll make it up to you once the crisis lifts." They did, and we made good on our promise. We not only got through the hard times, the company began to grow. The moral of this story: when in doubt, go for full disclosure, and do your business out in the open in the guileless way that all dogs do.

The Key to Training Dogs and People: Release Their Natural Enthusiasm

Most enlightened animal trainers don't try to force their will on a dog. Instead, they channel the creature's natural enthusiasm. "We don't punish. We don't go in for dominance," Susan Tripp, founder of the Animal Behavior Network, a resource for people who own and work with animals in need of retraining, said in an interview. "We find out what an animal likes doing, and then reward it, and subtly guide it so it performs to the best of its ability." Dogs trained this way are astonishingly creative and adaptive and much more likely to outperform their peers.

If you apply these same principles at the office, you can produce a new caliber of employee—one who doesn't only respond to commands but also is capable of making independent choices. Many of the executives profiled in *The New York Times* column "Corner Office" are now doing this instinctively.

When Joseph Plumeri took over Willis Group Holdings as chairman and CEO, he decided not to bring in a new management team, but instead opted to empower the people who were already there. He found out what they were good at and then encouraged them to develop those strengths.

"There's a presumption that a new CEO comes into a bad company and gets rid of everybody," Plumeri told *The New York Times*. "I believe you can actually get people to do things they never believed they could do with the right motivation. For the first five years I didn't replace a single person at the executive level. Once I got them over the hill, I really had some converts. When you see [people] over the hill, they're maniacal." Plumeri isn't reinventing the wheel. He's simply using the principles of positive reinforcement, which anyone can do.

Mindy Grossman, CEO of retailer HSN (The Home Shopping Network), gets results by finding out what makes her employees passionate about their jobs, and then giving them regular strokes or "treats." She told *The New York Times*, "I learn as much from the boy in backstage TV as I do from my CFO. Anybody can e-mail me. I do town halls with employees at least once every eight weeks and I have lunch every month with people who have celebrated five-, ten-, fifteen-, and twenty-five-year anniversaries." On these occasions, she asks, "Why are you here, and why are you staying?" Grossman said she likes to hire "energy givers"—people with a doglike level of enthusiasm—because they help others to do their best work.

Then there's Jeffrey Katzenberg, CEO of DreamWorks Animation, who apprenticed under two difficult bosses. Katzenberg knows you won't get far with the controlling, punitive approach. Bosses like this tend to break your spirit, just as an overly controlling trainer tends to break a dog's.

So Katzenberg gives his staff as much creative freedom as they can handle and believes that a CEO should be a facilitator not a dictator. "You cannot surround yourself with the smartest and most talented people and then start looking over your shoulder, worried that someone smarter or better might be on your heels," he said. The most important thing, he added, is making people feel secure.

First Safety, Then Creativity

One thing I can tell you from long experience: animals—of any kind—won't do anything if they feel threatened or afraid. A dog will simply dig in its heels and become "untrainable." Under stress, people will also shut down and grow more risk averse. They won't dare to try new things or think outside the box. And pretty soon, they'll bring your operation to a grinding halt.

Just as trainers give a dog freedom to experiment and get things wrong, a CEO needs to give his staff permission to fail. I always tell my people as they begin a project: "If you're trying and then not discarding at least five new ideas, you're not trying hard enough." In a tight economy, people are even more likely to seize up and be wary of trying new approaches. But as every business leader knows, the moment you stop being creative, you're all washed up.

As a manager, your job is to get your employees to relax so they can focus on what they do best, rather than spend valuable time worrying about reprisal if they happen to veer off track. In fact, your approach is similar to that of a good dog trainer— point people in the right direction, then instill trust and confidence.

If your staff members come up with a radical idea, loosen the leash and let them run with it. In dog training, the word "no" doesn't work—it just frustrates the animal. The same is true for people. You have to make each project a learning experience that contributes to an employee's growth.

When I'm addressing a group of CEOs and other managers, I ask, "Do you want to motivate your staff and release their full creative potential?" As they begin to nod, I read them three simple rules and tell them to replace the word "dog" with "people." First, identify your dogs' strengths and find out what engages them and keeps them energized. Next, learn to channel their natural exuberance. Finally, remember that dogs are eminently social creatures *who respond to our belief in them.*

The Myth of the Alpha Leader

The next thing I tell business leaders usually comes as a shock: Don't try to be the alpha dog. In the wild, dogs have a much more fluid approach to leadership, and exchange roles as needed. Recent animal research shows that the pack doesn't spend each moment fighting for control and dominance. Darwin noted that evolution favors flexibility and collaboration. Dogs have mastered this.

My friend and colleague Dr. Alan Beck, who researches the human-animal bond at Purdue University, said it's never been a dog-eat-dog world. "We have assumed that there's a single animal in charge of the pack, but in the wild, leadership changes with the situation. The good hunter takes over when the pack is in pursuit of prey. If the job is taking care of the young, another animal takes charge. Command isn't frozen or static. It's whoever's best at the task at hand."

What does this mean for CEOs today? The old command-and-control model of leadership is based on our own projections and on a serious misunderstanding of how things work in nature. A pack can, and often does, function smoothly without an alpha dog. So can an organization. A CEO still needs to guide the daily operations, but in healthy companies, there is more give-and-take between the leader and the troops.

In each job I've had over the past twenty years, I've refused the role of alpha dog and have relied instead on a pack-like model of collaboration. The industry association I run today has a virtually flat organizational chart. There are no spikes or pinnacles, special perks, or fancy titles. Everything we do is team-based. We have a task force to handle our trade show, our membership, and our public relations. Staff members are briefed on all aspects of our work in weekly meetings. I contribute to each project, often working side by side with junior employees. There's an advantage to this kind of canine collaboration: if you do a little of everything, you don't fall out of the loop on anything. And when there's a problem, you get instant feedback. The pack model has never let me down—and I'm pleased to report that more and more CEOs are converting to it.

"I was once a command-and-control guy but the environment's different," Joseph Plumeri, former chairman, president, and CEO of Willis Group, told *The New York Times*. "I think now it's a question of making people feel they're making a contribution and they're part of the process. In the end, you're still directing the process, but you're allowing for the collaboration and debate to take place." Plumeri, like many other leaders, now sees his role as that of a facilitator, not a top-down commander.

William Green, chairman and former CEO of Accenture, a consulting, technology services, and outsourcing company, also believes power sharing is vital to a company's success. "Nothing today is about the individual," he said in a recent interview. "It's all about the team and in the end, about giving a damn about your customers, your company, and the people around you."

A Canine Model of Power Sharing

Smart CEOs run the workplace like a dog pack. When hiring, they look for people with that doglike sense of loyalty and service. These folks are much more likely to put the welfare of the group above their own egos and ambitions.

When recruiting at Babson College in 1991, Green recalled interviewing a student who didn't list any clubs, sports, or extracurricular activities on his résumé. It was Green's last appointment that day. He was tired, and the conversation looked like it could easily be a waste of time. But when an eager face appeared before him, Green wanted to give the young man a chance. He asked, "What else were you doing here at college?" The candidate responded, "Sam's Diner. That's our family business. I leave on Friday after classes and I work until closing. I work all day Saturday until closing, and then I work all day Sunday and drive back to school." Green was impressed by the young man's loyalty and persever- ance, and hired him to work at Accenture, where he's still employed today. But what struck Green the most was that this young man was a team player. There was nothing he wouldn't do—from serving to washing dishes to cleaning up—to make his parents' diner a success.

The good news is that young people just en- tering the workforce are far more comfortable with this canine model of collaboration. A report by the Institute for the Future in Palo Alto, California, in- dicates that members of Generations X and Y aren't fixated on getting to the corner office. Most of them consider hierarchy to be both arrogant and outdated. Instead, they prefer the pack model and an informal chain of command where they feel free to express their points of view.

We baby boomers are a different breed. We wanted to succeed on our own merits and, if the boss assigned someone to help us, we took this as a sign that he was displeased with our work. But Generations X and Y have grown up with the collaborative power of the Internet; they get peer input on every aspect of their lives, from how to handle an accounting job or create a new software program, to the music they listen to and the places they shop. This is what it's like in a dog pack as well. Each member is giving constant cues and feedback to the others. The emphasis is on sharing skills and information.

Savvy managers understand that the upcoming generations won't respond to the old "line model," but will instead prefer the loose pack-like affiliation. They allow their younger employees to shift roles and share responsibilities as they see fit, and in the long run, it's easier on a CEO. For one thing, it's not as critical to put your top person on every project. If they don't know the answer, members of Generation X will reach out to their colleagues and get the needed expertise.

I have to remind my younger workers of only one thing: each job is equally important. "When you start this project," I say, "you have no idea what's going to derail you. The best way to guard against this is to remember that every person's contribution is critical. If any one of you gets confused and screws up, everybody suffers. So be like good sled dogs and pull the load together."

Today we're seeing this kind of power sharing at the very top because a chief executive has many roles to fill. A leader has to be a marketing maven, technology genius, and futurist, as well as a detail-oriented person who keeps track of day-to-day operations. There are usually several candidates, each with different skill sets, competing for the job. Boards and search committees may take months to choose, and often wish that they could combine the talents of their two top applicants. Once again, the dog world gives us an intriguing model of collaboration.

When a friend of mine introduced a young doberman into a household that already had three dogs and four cats, the result was instant chaos. Right away the newcomer challenged the leader, an even-tempered Labrador. The Lab had inherited her position as head of the pack and didn't want to fight. Yet the doberman edged into the Lab's territory, trying to displace the leader from the prime spot at the foot of their master's bed. For a while, my friend had to separate the dogs and feared she'd have to get rid of the newcomer or face a fatal dog fight. Yet the next time they squared off, the Lab did something completely unexpected: instead of protecting her turf at the foot of the bed, she stepped aside and made room for the doberman. From then on, they shared the best and highest sleeping place in the house. In the dog world, this is an indication that you've adopted your rival as a family member. The newcomer got the status that she craved; from then on, the two dogs ruled the pack together.

The American anthropologist Elizabeth Marshall Thomas tells a similar story about a feisty Australian dingo she adopted. If you've ever wondered what goes on inside a dog's head, Marshall's tale is proof that they, too, rely on dreams to work things out. After a particularly nasty encounter with the aggressive newcomer, Thomas' older dog, Pearl, started twitching and barking in her sleep as if she were getting ready for a fight. But this rehearsal for battle turned out to be too stressful for her. In the end, she decided it was better to make room for the dingo at her bowl on the kitchen floor and broker an alliance with her. Thomas was extremely grateful as her household went back to normal, thanks to Pearl's generosity.

In general, female dogs are more willing to stand down and share power, which is what happened when Amy Pascal was asked to share the reins at Sony Pictures Entertainment with Michael Lynton, a company outsider. This is a story that, by now, everyone knows well. Pascal was in line to take the top position, but, at the last minute, the board decided to bring in someone new. At the time, Lynton was head of AOL Europe, and the board felt he could help the company expand internationally.

Pascal had a lot of strengths: she'd served as president of Columbia Pictures, a division of Sony, and had a reputation for backing successful films, including *When Harry Met Sally* and *A League of Their Own*. A product of the middle class, Pascal had attended the University of California, and was steeped in popular culture. Born into a wealthy family and raised in the Netherlands, Lynton had attended Harvard and worked on Wall Street.

Pascal saw film as a means of inspiring a new generation to reach for their dreams, while Lynton thought Sony could no longer be just a place that turned out movies and television shows. In his view, Sony needed to focus on future opportunities, such as developing digital hardware that would bring new content to consumers. These two executives couldn't have been more different.

Eventually they fashioned a relationship as inspired as the one worked out by the old Lab. Over time, Pascal and Lynton developed an almost familial bond. They went to the same synagogue, shared the same architect, and sent their children to the same schools. "It's unique because we treat our partnership like a relationship," Pascal told *The New York Times*, adding that this is something "two men would find hard to do." Sony is now viewed as one of the more stable companies in the entertainment industry. To survive, Sony chairman Howard Stringer observed, studios need to move past the egos and flamboyance associated with old Hollywood.

This story also reminds us that a corporation is not just a means of making money, but is also a place of belonging and affiliation. While each dog might wish to be number one, most of them value membership in the group over dominance. As animal behavior expert Elizabeth Marshall Thomas notes, they would rather be part of a social system that's solid, firm, and dependable, like a good strong ladder.

People need a similar environment in the workplace. Without a sense of belonging, your workers will grow anxious and your company will contract. Once again, it comes down to canine wisdom: there doesn't need to be an alpha dog. We can share responsibilities and create a solid social ladder that's inclusive and can hold every member of the pack.

The Dog vs. the Lone Wolf

Rogue CEOs are less like dogs and more like lone wolves. Why? Because they've broken the social contract and failed to consider the best interests of the pack. For this reason they are shunned. I don't mean to give wolves a bad name. As the direct ancestors of the dog, they are highly social creatures, often mate for life, and have strong bonding rituals. The lone wolf, however, is in a dangerous situation because he lacks the support and protection of the group. He thus has to be extremely careful when he wanders into unknown or unfamiliar territory.

I witnessed the consequences of lone wolf behavior firsthand in 1983, when my company, Union Carbide, had to deal with a toxin spill in Bhopal, India. Although I was in the consumer division, not the chemical division, I was distressed by the way our CEO, Warren Anderson, dealt with this traumatic news. As the board worried about stock prices, Anderson took a lone wolf posture, denying responsibility for the contaminated water supply and a reported 15,000 deaths. I personally feel that he was badly briefed and would have reacted differently if he'd had all the facts. But by failing to stand by the community in which his company operated, Anderson broke the social contract and exposed both himself and his firm to years of litigation and attack. In the best-case scenario, this CEO would have told the people of Bhopal, "We're trying to find out what happened and then we'll do everything we can to help."

When BP's Tony Hayward took a similar lone wolf approach to capping the oil well in the Louisiana Gulf in 2010, he was roundly criticized for stonewalling and failing to reach out to government agencies, according to *The New York Times*. Across the board—in the fields of finance, environmental management, and product manufacturing—CEOs have made the same mistake. Going rogue is a risky proposition. Stay too long in that liminal state where you're cut off from the pack and you'll join the ranks of those who are labeled heartless, inept, crazy, or just plain profiteers.

In the late 1990s, CEOs in America were acting like lone wolves when they initiated predatory pricing. "This practice started as a means to undercut the competition but it ended up harming the whole ecology," W. Stanton Smith, a former partner at the global consulting and accounting firm Deloitte & Touche, said in an interview. "Everyone lost money, and everyone had less work to do." Once business and consumers got used to the words "cut-rate" and "introductory discount," they saw no reason to go back to paying full price for the same services. Lone wolf behavior had changed the game.

Customers are now used to getting a free ride, and some economists believe that predatory pricing set the stage for the Great Recession. In fact, it was as deadly a miscalculation as the manipulation of sub-prime mortgage rates.

For the past century, Darwin's notion of the "survival of the fittest" has fed a winner-takes-all mentality. In nineteenth-century Europe it was used to justify ruthless competition and empire building. Yet nature does not favor competition over cooperation. As our institutions grow more humane, they begin to emulate the dog, with its collaborative instincts, rather than the lone wolf.

The lesson for CEOs and all managers is this: if you see cooperation as a weakness, you're more likely to engage in cut-rate practices that will eventually put you out of business. The lone wolf doesn't give us a sustainable business model. To succeed, we have to be good guard dogs, consider the welfare of the pack, and extend that care to the community.

When the economy took a downward turn in 2009, many companies made drastic cuts in the rank and file while leaving upper management intact. In the wild, a dog pack shares the resources when times are good, and, when times are bad, they share the sacrifice. American workers were dismayed when their leaders did nothing of the sort.

In lean periods, those in top management ought to trim their own salaries and trim their ranks as well. Instead of keeping all their perks, senior managers ought to tell their workers, "We all have to make some sacrifices. And when things pick up, we'll share the benefits across the board."

The trouble is, as companies keep downsizing, they keep cutting jobs from the bottom of the pyramid. According to a 2010 report by the Institute for Policy Studies, "CEO Pay and the Great Recession," the fifty firms that have laid off the most workers since the onset of the economic crisis rewarded their CEOs with nearly $12 million in 2009. These fifty organizations eliminated 531,363 jobs despite reporting a 44 percent average profit increase. Even more astonishing is the proportionate increase in executive pay. After adjusting for inflation, CEO compensation in 2009 was more than double the average in the 1990s, more than quadruple the average for the 1980s, and eight times the average for all the decades in the mid-twentieth century. Meanwhile, American workers are taking home less money in real dollars than they earned in the 1970s. This is the result of "the rule of the lone wolf."

Many of these mega-corporations would have gone belly up without government bailouts. Small and midsize firms can't afford to follow suit. The bottom line: you won't have a company to run if you lay off the people who can build your products and provide your basic services. Sooner or later someone will realize that you're an ineffective leader, and then another wolf will be at your throat.

Your Main Job: Protecting the Pack

It's far better to be a good sled dog. This is the most powerful draft animal on earth. A group of twenty can match a team of horses and they're much faster over the long haul. There is no hierarchy here; sled dogs cover great distances, conquering difficult and dangerous terrain, because they work together. Dogs like this helped us settle the Alaskan wilderness, carrying our supplies and replacing the Pony Express. In *Call of the Wild*, Jack London pays homage to a sled dog's stamina and heroism. When I was a kid, I thought this was the greatest adventure story ever told. A cross between a Saint Bernard and a collie, Buck is kidnapped from a comfortable home in Pasadena and sold to trappers in Alaska. His new masters beat him and force him to carry heavy loads, yet he gains the trust of the other dogs, and together, they set a record for the fastest mail run across the Alaskan territory. Finally, he's adopted by an old prospector who treats him kindly. This man boasts about his dog's strength and stamina and rashly bets all his worldly goods that Buck can haul a sled weighing half a ton. As the whole town gathers to watch this contest, the dog struggles to break the runners free of icy ground. At the crucial moment, his master leans down and whispers, "As you love me, Buck." As the dog surges forward, his haunches glistening, each muscle rippling, and finally moves the load, people run beside him and cheer him on. I tell this story because it shows what we love best about dogs: their extraordinary capacity for love and devotion. A CEO would be fortunate, indeed, to summon up this loyalty in his people, and to be able to count on such a willingness to serve.

Yet *Call of the Wild* also shows us what happens when we take this love for granted. In many ways this book is a cautionary tale that also illustrates the perils of mismanagement. Jack London gives us a stark portrait of what happens when a dog like Buck falls into the hands of inexperienced leaders. Earlier in the book, a group of settlers sets out late in the season with too heavy a load. They have no knowledge of the wilderness, so they fail to ration their food. As winter sets in, the dogs begin to starve. By the time they reach the next outpost, half of the dogs are dead. The old-timers advise the group to stop so the remaining dogs can rest. But the next morning, the settlers harness up and force the team across a frozen river. The team balks, sensing danger. Their leader whips them out onto the ice, and there is a sudden crack as both men and dogs are pulled down underneath the floes.

I often invoke this tale, warning CEOs not to push the rank and file too hard. In tough times, managers often fail to care for their most dedicated workers just as these miners failed to care for their dogs. Right now we're asking more from the labor force than ever. In 2006, economist Sylvia Ann Hewlett charted the rise of "extreme jobs" that required workers to put in sixty hours a week or more. "In large corporations," she reported, "almost half of high-echelon workers had 'extreme jobs.'" The result was a dramatic increase in stress-related illnesses. We were literally working our best people into the ground. During the Great Recession, the time squeeze tightened even more. By now few people dare to ask if they can stagger their hours or work a day or two from home. Many fear that being out of the office means that they will be invisible and that during the next round of cuts, they'll be the first to go. In contrast, some of the most successful firms have recently begun using both flextime and time off to attract and retain a high-performing staff. In 2009, the accounting giant KPMG initiated a program called Flexible Futures that allowed their workers in Britain to drop down to a four-day workweek with a 20 percent pay cut, or take a short sabbatical while receiving 30 percent of their usual pay. Booz & Company took a similar approach, offering employees a one- to twelve-month sabbatical at 20 percent of their base salary. Workers keep their medical benefits and, after the agreed-upon time, return to secure jobs.

Members of Generation Y are willing to work 24/7 to meet crucial deadlines, but they also expect downtime once the project is finished, according to a report by the Institute for the Future. This is, essentially, a canine rhythm: a pack endures extreme deprivation when it's hunting for food, then it rests. Members of Generations X and Y are determined to avoid the kind of burnout they've witnessed in their parents and are much more concerned with work-life balance. The challenge for managers today is to come up with a way of judging performance that's not based on hours spent at the office, but on contribution to the bottom line. Still, the message is the same:

when jobs may be here today and gone tomorrow, a doglike sense of loyalty may be the difference between success and failure.

Hire People Who Have a Doglike Passion

Verlyn Klinkenborg, writing in *The New York Times*, described the boundless energy and dedication of sled dogs. As the men slow their pace, "the dogs, seven of them, attached to the harness—look impatiently at us, haunches quivering, ready to pull and pull again. We have been sledding down an old portage road, along the lip of a beaver dam, through a runnel of young white birch, onto the open ice... and I find myself wondering, why do sled dogs run? It is not a matter of driving them. All the work is in pacing them, restraining them. When my friend Murphy stands on the brake, the gang line quivers with tension. The dogs torque forward again before he can shout, 'Let's go!'"

I often tell CEOs, "Look for people with a doglike enthusiasm for work and your company will never falter." Fred Seddiqui, CEO of Silicon Valley Venture Partners, agreed. "My main job," he said in an interview, "is finding people with enough stamina to keep on going and enough intelligence to meet our goals." Every CEO serves as a kind of "chief endurance officer." But it's the team that takes him to the finish line. So assemble the best sled team you can find, and work beside them. Your company depends on your team's natural vitality and strength.

Jeff Swartz, president and CEO of Timberland, has said that he looks for these doglike qualities when he interviews prospective hires. He even asks each candidate, "What makes you howl at the moon?" knowing that employees who have this kind of passion and commitment allow a CEO to soar.

Chapter 2

What Breed of Manager
Are You?

When President Barack Obama took office in 2009, I wondered how his choice of a dog might reflect his approach to governing. The Portuguese water dog is highly intelligent and energetic; it makes a fine guardian yet would rather build consensus than attack. So far, that's an accurate description of Obama's operating style.

This got me thinking about America's leaders, both business and political. Steve Jobs, Henry Kravis, Sam Walton, Michael Bloomberg, and Martha Stewart are all at the top of their professions, but when you look at how they run their companies, you see that they are different animals with specific strengths and flaws.

As breeders know, each type of dog has unique qualities. Sled dogs, like huskies and malamutes, are the closest to the wolf—they are less "people-oriented" and more self-contained. Labs and golden retrievers are "people pleasers" and always at their owners' heels. Terriers are tenacious, while poodles are savvy and aloof. And while bird dogs have a single focus, herders like the border collie have amazing peripheral vision and know what's going on with every member of the group. In short, temperament is everything. As the American psychoanalyst Smiley Blanton once said, "Things that upset a terrier may pass virtually unnoticed by a Great Dane."

My coauthor and I observed distinctive canine traits among our leading CEOs and managers. We later developed a test, "What Breed Are You?" to help you discover which of these top dogs you most resemble. Simply answer yes or no to the following questions, then we'll tell you about the canine talents you share with well-known corporate leaders.

Top Dog #1

1. Will you eagerly challenge a bigger and more successful opponent?
2. Do you tend to bark out your ideas and be extremely vocal—even when you're on somebody else's turf?
3. Do you refuse to roll over for others if you think you have a better plan?
4. Do you follow your own instincts and find it hard to take direction?
5. Do others sometimes find you a bit controlling or aggressive?

Top Dog #2

1. Do you use humor to motivate others?
2. Do you approach your work as play?
3. Are you good at reading the body language and emotional cues of your co-workers?
4. Do you take the time to learn about your colleagues' personal lives?
5. Does your staff sometimes feel overwhelmed or have trouble matching your level of enthusiasm?

Top Dog #3

1. Do you pride yourself on being both a facilitator and a leader?
2. Are you good at moving others toward consensus?
3. Do people see you as the ultimate decision maker?
4. Are you adaptable to change?
5. Do your team members ever accuse you of micromanaging; i.e., nipping at their heels to be sure the job gets done?

Top Dog #4

1. Once you set a course, are you unlikely to back down?
2. When confronted with a crisis, do you first explore the tried-and-true solutions?
3. Are you always mindful of company traditions?
4. Do you see your primary role as protecting market share or defending the status quo?
5. Do people sometimes find you a little gruff or overly defensive?

Top Dog #5

1. Do you do your best work when you're alone?
2. Is independent thinking more important to you than reaching a consensus?
3. Are you the marathon runner in your group, known for your ability to go the distance and to tackle the most demanding projects?
4. Do you prefer the thrill of R&D over administrative tasks?
5. Do your peers ever complain that you're too much of a lone wolf?

Top Dog #6

1. Do you often surprise people with your extensive knowledge on a topic?

2. Do you like to shake things up and steer a meeting in a new and unexpected direction?

3. Do you put a high premium on personal loyalty and tend to choose employees who can be counted on to carry out your wishes?

4. Are you a quick study, able to digest new information readily but at the same time easily bored?

5. Do colleagues sometimes view you as aloof or unapproachable?

Top Dog #7

1. Do you tend to wander far and wide, going beyond your usual territory to find new products or alliances?

2. Are you able to sniff out solutions to those hard-core problems that stymie most of your colleagues?

3. When you hit an obstacle, do you usually find a way around it?

4. Do you stubbornly defend your point of view, even if there's no one else to back you?

5. Are you so highly focused when you're on the hunt for new business or a new idea that you simply ignore everything else?

Now tally the times you answered yes to the questions in each category. If you identified strongly with two or more categories, that's good news. That means you're a mongrel, with the best characteristics of several breeds. And that makes you one of the more versatile managers or CEOs.

If you identify with Top Dog #1, you're a Tenacious Terrier, like fashion magnate Diane von Furstenberg, Fox broadcasting mogul Barry Diller, media mogul Rupert Murdoch, and Silicon Valley entrepreneur Larry Ellison.

Strengths: You're a scrappy, independent leader. You're the small dog who eagerly takes on bigger and stronger competitors. You know what you want and you go for the deal, no matter how high the stakes.

One interesting thing I've learned about small dogs like the terrier: people are attracted to them because they're cute and baby-like, yet this doesn't make them harmless. While their genetic traits and appearance is the farthest from the wolf (compared to the husky or the malamute), these dogs actually behave more like wolf pups than any other breed. In the wild, wolf pups are allowed to nip and bite and be far more aggressive than their elders. This is nature's way of ensuring their survival. But as these young wolves mature, they develop the submissive traits necessary to live harmoniously in groups. A terrier is thus behaving like an immature wolf cub when he challenges a bigger dog and refuses to back down. He has yet to learn how to diplomatically defer to other members of the pack.

The word "terrier" comes from the Latin word *terra*, meaning "of the earth," since these dogs were bred to rid the land of moles and garden pests. They attack the ground with great fury, tunneling with their hind legs, and mercilessly rout their prey. If you're a terrier, you are likely to have a kind of tunnel vision—the ability to block out everything except for your primary goal.

Weaknesses: You can be aggressive and overly dominant. But your bark is usually worse than your bite. People who know you well give you lots of latitude and know that you are fiercely driven and intensely focused. Your motto is "Never give up," no matter what the odds against you. But you're not approachable; your raw, primal energy is intimidating and tends to keep others at bay. Balance out your management style by studying the golden retriever or, better yet, hire one as your second-in-command. You need a "people pleaser" to smooth things over and keep the business running smoothly day to day.

Best of breed: Terriers like Oracle's Larry Ellison never give up—that quality is bred in the bone. Ellison was born to a nineteen-year-old single mother in the Bronx, then raised by relatives on the South Side of Chicago. When his adoptive father lost his real estate business in the Great Depression and took a menial job, Ellison determined never to settle for second best. In 1977, he founded a software company, designing a database for the CIA. The firm went public in 1986. When its stock price fell, Ellison turned over the financial management and concentrated solely on the product, leading to a strong recovery. His drive spilled over into sports, and he gained a reputation as a mountain biker and body surfer. After an injury, Ellison diverted his energies, becoming an aerobatic pilot and then a sailor. As captain of the Oracle yacht the *Rising Sun*, he raced through hurricane winds and won the America's Cup in 2010. I can think of no other CEO with more grit and determination. Oracle is now the largest business software company, serving the top 100 companies on *Fortune* magazine's Global 500 list.

CEOs like Ellison gravitate to areas where they can excel. If one avenue is blocked, they'll find another that is more advantageous and that allows them to show off their considerable skills. At the core of this breed is a dogged determination not to fail and a singleness of purpose that borders on compulsion. It's pointless to disagree with a terrier, and at times, the dialogue may deteriorate into a shouting match. But they also know when to ask for help and how to reach out to others with complementary strengths.

Designer Diane von Furstenberg is of the same feisty breed. Though she has been described as a mix of sex kitten and tiger, she's a terrier at heart—fiercely competitive with a sharp bark. When the cut-price chains of Target and Forever 21 did knockoffs of her dress designs, she sued. She also railed against the prevalence of ultra-skinny fashion models and lobbied the fashion industry to put women of different racial and cultural backgrounds on runways and magazine covers. Like all terriers, she has tenacity and staying power: she introduced her wrap dress in 1975, then enjoyed success a second time around with an updated version that she now markets in China. Von Furstenberg is married to fellow terrier Barry Diller, the media mogul behind *The Daily Beast*, and she has been a longtime supporter of yet another of her breed, Hillary Clinton, who doggedly pushed herself through a grueling primary campaign for the presidency. Furstenberg's memorable Tenacious Terrier quotation is, "Attitude is everything."

If you identify with Top Dog #2, you're a Golden Retriever, like former president Bill Clinton, former Hewlett-Packard CEO Carly Fiorina, venture capitalist John Doerr, and yours truly.

Strengths: You're the boss everybody loves: a good-natured and people-oriented person who's also a terrific judge of character. You read body language and emotional cues extremely well, making you a natural leader and a top-notch motivator. You do well in sales or service positions that require ongoing contact with the public. You're a great spokesperson and will enhance the reputation of your company or product.

Weaknesses: You're so energetic that you can easily overwhelm your staff and drive them to exhaustion. Learn from the border collie about how to properly pace the herd.

Best of breed: Known for his almost superhuman energy and endurance, venture capitalist John Doerr has backed some of the most innovative companies in the world, including Amazon, Compaq, Google, Intuit, Netscape, and Sun Microsystems. These start-ups have created more than 150,000 jobs. As a partner at Kleiner Perkins Caufield & Byers in Menlo Park, California, Doerr has had an unerring nose for identifying future industries and leaders. A well-known philanthropist, he has served on the board of NewSchools Venture Fund, promoting charter schools, and is now supporting clean energy. He's always out there gathering solutions—then putting his money behind the ones most likely to succeed. Like all golden retrievers, Doerr is service-oriented: "People [in Silicon Valley] are looking to have more meaning in their lives," he said. "It is a sign the technology community is coming of age."

Carly Fiorina is another retriever who rose to the top on her extraordinary people skills. In her first leadership position, she brought Lucent, an AT&T communications equipment spin-off, into a modern world with a $90 million brand-building campaign. Impressed by her star personality and her marketing expertise, Hewlett-Packard wooed her away. She managed to turn this outfit with a reputation for stodginess into a leading purveyor of Internet technology, reorganizing the chain of command and reducing the bureaucracy. After HP merged with the computer giant Compaq, Fiorina promised to use company profits to help poor communities around the world. A proponent of human rights, this former philosophy major envisioned the role of the corporation in society as a guardian for those in need.

When the company's stock price began to drop, HP needed a hands-on CEO who would focus on its day-to-day operations. As a retriever, Fiorina was used to reeling people in and convincing them to play with her. Tracking nuts and bolts of manufacturing wasn't her main strength. At this point in her career, she might have chosen a detail-oriented border collie or a highly focused husky as her second-in-command.

If you analyze her speeches, you see that what Fiorina enjoyed most was bringing disparate groups together. In her 2004 commencement address to the California Institute of Technology, she said, "The Silicon Valley of the twentieth century has given way to the scientific canyon of the twenty-first century, with scientists on one side, the general public on the other, and too few guides who can help bring us safely across from one side to the other." She hoped to be that bridge.

If you identify with Top Dog #3, you're a Border Collie, like Wal-Mart founder Sam Walton, lifestyle maven Martha Stewart, and Yahoo's Carol Bartz.

Strengths: The border collie has it all; smarts, independence, and the ability to get the best from others. This breed is a natural CEO. If this is your type, you combine the best qualities of the lone wolf with the ability to collaborate and motivate others.

Weaknesses: Few. As a leader, you can be anxious and demanding, but you're also protective of your pack and extremely loyal. You push them hard but you also reward your people for their service. My only advice: don't exhaust yourself by running all over the map.

Best of breed: When it comes to border collies, Sam Walton easily wins Best in Show. Known for his collaborative management style, Walton kept his customers happy by offering lower prices (thanks to discounts from wholesalers) and by staying open longer hours. He kept employees happy by introducing a profit-sharing plan and rewarding good performance. He was clearly listening to his inner dog when he said, "Individuals don't win, teams do." The largest retailer in the world, Wal-Mart had a database second only to the Pentagon's. But Sam Walton was personally involved in the launching of each new mega-store and enjoyed scouting out new locations in his private plane. A good border collie, he herded the American population into the mall and led the entire retail industry into the discount age, paving the way for other giants like Barnes & Noble, the Home Depot, and Blockbuster. He also did so without drawing attention to himself—almost no one had heard of Sam Walton when *Forbes* magazine first named him "the richest man in America" in 1985. Some of his best border collie wisdom: "If you love your work, you'll be out there every day trying to do it the best you possibly can, and pretty soon everybody around will catch the passion from you—like a fever."

Martha Stewart is another example of the tireless herder. After a modeling career and a stint as a stockbroker, Stewart started a catering business from her nineteenth-century farm, in Westport, Connecticut, and eventually built a media and retail empire. With more than 650 employees, she has become an expert in human resources. Many of her current staff members have been with her from the beginning, and all have the same passion and cheery "do-it-yourself" optimism associated with her brand. Stewart's strength is her ability to get the best from others. When she was caught up in an SEC case, she confidently handed her company over to the team she'd trained and vetted, then returned to build her business into an even more successful one. Like a good border collie, Martha Stewart is able to lead the pack in a new direction. Typical border collie wisdom: What worked well last month may suddenly not be working at all. People change, companies change, and it is only the successful manager who is able to reconcile the two.

If you identify with Top Dog #4, you're a Rottweiler, or a corporate protector, who preserves a legacy, like Max De Pree and Michael Volkema, former CEOs of Herman Miller, and Anne Mulcahy, former CEO of Xerox.

Strengths: You're the kind of leader who sets a course of action and sees it through. You're not likely to squander company resources on ideas that have little chance of succeeding. You value tradition, and you look to the past for lessons that might help you to deal with a crisis. You're cautious and not easily seduced by new ideas.

Weaknesses: A good protector often ends up as the "old guard" once the younger generation comes along. You need to cultivate the independence of the husky and the courage of the terrier to move into the future. Your challenge is to listen to the innovators and to learn to lead—not just respond to industry change.

Best of breed: What should you do when you inherit a company or have to inject new life into a well-known brand? Build on a firm's reputation for quality and service. In the early 1960s, Max De Pree took over the company, then called Herman Miller Furniture, from his father and started working with top designers like Ray and Charles Eames. The younger De Pree instituted a bold profit-sharing plan, and Herman Miller was soon known as one of America's most socially responsible businesses. It soon landed on the Fortune 500 list of most profitable companies, ranking seventh in terms of total return to investors. Max De Pree summarized his brand of forward-thinking guardianship in his book *Leadership Is an Art* and later turned over the reins to Dick Ruck. Then from 1995 to 2004, some visionary changes were made by his successor, Michael Volkema. Under Volkema, the company entered a new era of growth. It started shipping 25,000 of its ergonomic Aeron chairs a week, the Museum of

Modern Art bought one in its permanent collection, and Malcolm Gladwell praised the design in his best-seller, *Blink: The Power of Thinking Without Thinking*.

But soon the company was facing major challenges. During the dot-com bust in 2000, sales of office furniture dropped to a new low. After sustaining losses of $56 million, Volkema invested an almost equal amount in R&D, introducing "systems furniture" for cubicles, a new environmentally friendly chair, a sound muffling system, and SQA (simple, quick, affordable) office modules. Along the way he had to shut down the company's plant in Georgia, and sell some of its real estate, including a Frank Gehry building. Volkema's best rottweiler wisdom: "Leadership is about doing the right thing, not the easy thing."

If you identify with Top Dog #5, you're a Husky, or an independent thinker, like Steve Jobs, CEO of Apple, and A.G. Lafley, former CEO of Procter & Gamble.

Strengths: The husky and all the northern breeds are serenely independent and perform with little direction from above. If you identify with this breed, you're exceptionally strong and hardworking, and able to carry a heavy load. Huskies, because of their stamina and dogged perseverance, are ideal researchers and financial managers.

Weaknesses: Huskies have a tendency to roam and to follow their own impulses if not fenced in. If you're a husky, you'll need to learn how to check with colleagues to make sure you have their support for your boundless creativity. My best advice: don't neglect to build consensus. Learn from the golden or the border collie, or hire one to be your interface with senior management. If you're managing a husky, you'll have to do a balancing act: give them their space to pursue their dreams and, at the same time, set clear limits.

Best of breed: Huskies are the perfect heads of R&D. We wouldn't have any of our fun tools and gadgets without them. Steve Jobs was always more excited about new technology than he was about making money—and that's probably the only thing that kept him from upstaging Microsoft's Bill Gates. In 1976, Jobs and his partner, Steve Wozniak, started Apple from a garage and sold their first personal computer for $666.66. In the years since, Jobs founded Pixar, the animation studio that produced the animated features *Up* and *Finding Nemo*, and revolutionized the music business with the iPod and iTunes. After his bout with pancreatic cancer, he furiously rolled out new applications for the iPad, which he calls a "truly magical alternative" to traditional books and periodicals. Here is Steve Jobs channeling his inner husky: "You can't just ask customers what they want and then try to give that to them. By the time you get it built, they'll want something new."

If you identify with Top Dog #6, you're a Poodle, an elegant but aloof leader, like financier Henry Kravis; businessman and New York City mayor

Michael Bloomberg; Microsoft's Bill Gates; and Avon's Chairman and CEO, Andrea Jung.

Strengths: Poodles are sensitive, thorough, highly energetic, and easily bored. They also like to shake things up. If you identify with this breed, you're best described as a quick study. Your intuition can be off the charts, and you're also a natural mischief-maker and may say or do astonishing things to move a meeting in a new direction. You'll always be an entertaining boss because you're open to change, and you inspire others with your overarching vision.

Weaknesses: Poodles tend to be the first to figure out a problem—they are astonishingly innovative. But this shrewdness and agility can sometimes work against them. If you're a poodle, you may leap ahead to the next problem before others have a chance to understand your thinking. As a leader, you may be seen as enigmatic or aloof. Smart poodles learn how to slow down and build consensus. They could take a lesson from the golden retriever and make sure they reach out to others. And when pushing for change, they make sure to give their co-workers a chance to get on board.

Best of breed: The perfect poodle, Henry Kravis is known for his glamorous parties and has always been drawn to the elegance of a deal. He invented the leveraged buyout so families could keep a stake in the businesses they founded and still continue in a management role. This solved an estate problem as well as a succession problem, and also allowed investors to make the tough decisions about how to streamline a company and tighten its budget. Kravis likes to hire other smart poodles: "I'm looking for people who are bright and have the highest ethical standards and will not compromise one iota," he has said. "I also want people who will stand up to me and aren't afraid to say exactly what's on their minds, though it's probably not what I'd like to hear."

If you identify with Top Dog #7, you're a Bloodhound, the kind of CEO or entrepreneur who can sniff out new ideas and cover an astounding range of territory. The bloodhound's sense of smell is up to 30,000 times stronger than an ordinary human's. This breed can follow a trail that is several days old and also distinguish the scent of one person from the next. Many leaders mentioned so far are at least part bloodhound: Steve Jobs, Bill Gates, A.G. Lafley, and Henry Kravis. These visionary CEOs used their sleuthing skills to transform the marketplace. At the beginning of their careers, all of them were bloodhounds—stubbornly following their noses and shutting everything else out until they came up with a business, and a formula, that worked.

Strengths: A bloodhound CEO can go beyond accepted boundaries and come up with products and services that no one has ever dreamed of. This breed also has great stamina and will follow a lead to the ends of the earth.

Weaknesses: The bloodhound's problem is knowing when to stop. This breed loves the thrill of the pursuit and will happily keep on chasing one lead after another. But while he's hot on the trail of some new project, who's going to keep things running smoothly day to day?

Best of breed: Sir Richard Branson, founder of Virgin Group, is perhaps the best example of this breed. Each year he seems to chase a new idea. He started out with a record company and ended up with a communications business (radio, television stations, books, computers, and video games), hotel chains, fitness centers, and a travel empire, which includes an international airline and a plan to shuttle tourists into outer space.

Fortunately Branson learned to delegate, hiring strong executives to head up each new venture. He also brought on a strong second-in-command, Stephen Murphy, as the company's global CEO to bring more discipline to his investments. Murphy's role was to nix some of Branson's more outlandish ideas and rein him in when necessary.

"I say no to him all the time," Murphy told *The Australian*, adding, "There are times when he ignores it, but he always listens." By protecting the company's best interests, Murphy acts as a good guard dog, and allows Branson to keep on doing what he loves best: sniffing out new ventures. He also has the expertise to test a new idea and bring it to fruition. This is a very savvy pairing of breeds with complementary strengths. As a result, Virgin is now moving into new territory—developing biofuels, solar panels, and alternative energy products—with clear business models and recognizable markets.

The Best CEOs Are Hybrids

Now that you've read these profiles, hopefully you know a bit more about your own "inner dog." You can also use these criteria to add new people to your management team, making sure you choose members who augment your natural strengths.

In my experience, most successful CEOs are hybrids, combining the best traits of two breeds. Veterinarians will tell you that such dogs are stronger, healthier, and more resilient than purebreds. Can't decide between a social retriever and a whip-smart poodle? Get a labradoodle. Want the added savvy and stamina of the border collie? Put your money on a bordoodle. The same is true for management styles: the more diverse your skills, the more effective you will be. So if you've tested high on at least two of these "Top Dog Profiles," you can pride yourself on being an unusually resourceful leader. George Bernard Shaw appreciated this kind of versatility. "I like a bit of a mongrel in myself," he said, "whether it's a man or a dog, it's best for every day."

No company is a one-dog show. As the role of chief executive becomes more complex, smart leaders will hire a strong second-in-command to complement their strengths. No matter which breed best describes you, you'll need to find colleagues who are trustworthy and embody a completely different set of strengths.

Different Breeds for Different Stages of a Company

One final note: as a company grows and changes, it may also require a different breed of leader. Silicon Valley entrepreneur and venture capitalist Randy Komisar has a theory about why most companies need to change CEOs as they evolve. The first CEO is the retriever, he told *Fast Company* magazine. "Leaders like this have to go out and assemble the resources. They have to find the people, the money, and the partners." They also have to be great sales-people because they have to sell the vision every day. "They're asking people to believe in something that doesn't exist and to take a substantial leap of faith."

The next to take charge of the pack is the blood-hound. "You've got to find out where the value is, so you can build a business around it. You've got some-thing, but how to you optimize it?" Komisar said. "You have to sleuth that out."

The bloodhound is followed by the husky, who takes over the R&D, and brings the product to the finish line. Komisar summed up this phase: "Now you've figured out your business model, and you've got to pull the sled, as it gets heavier with people, products, and customers."

The one dog you never want pulling your com-pany is the Saint Bernard. When you see the rescue dog, Komisar said, you know you're in big trouble. Think of the banks and the auto industry, with their management and assets all frozen in place until the government bailouts. My advice: run your business wisely and be sure to find the right breed of CEO to lead you through your current challenges. Leadership is a matter of applying the right kind of doggedness at the right time.

PART II

HOW TO WAG YOUR TAIL AT WORK

"The average dog is a nicer person than the average person."
—Andy Rooney

Chapter 3

Why the Pack Mentality Is Good for Business

A colleague once told me, "I'm the kind of person who keeps her nose down and stays completely focused on her work. How come I never get promoted?"

"Simple" I responded. "You don't know how to wag your tail at people yet."

My colleague had underestimated the role of the pack in the workplace. Studies show that the chief reason people decide to stay with a company is whether they feel connected to their coworkers and their boss. Humans, like dogs, want to be liked and accepted. More than anything else we want to feel that we belong.

That's why it's important for workers to have face time together, and to hang out at the company cafeteria, coffee machine, or watercooler.

"Most managers look at personal conversations among coworkers as a waste of company time," Charlice Hurst, a professor of organizational behavior at the University of Western Ontario, told *The Globe and Mail*. "But time spent this way can boost people's happiness on the job and benefit the organization." People need to bond with the other members of their pack. Professor Hurst studied 130 employees in sales and management, measuring their level of enthusiasm and positive feelings for their job after having brief interactions with coworkers. What mattered most to people was not the actual information they shared, but how warmly their colleagues reacted to their bits of news. When you receive an encouraging response from your coworkers, you feel that you have "family" at the office, and you'll then act in ways that benefit the organization.

"When I first started out at Coopers & Lybrand, the company had a strong pack-like atmosphere," W. Stanton Smith recalled. "Once you were accepted, you felt you'd be connected to those people for the rest of your life. And if you had a strong pack leader in your specialty, you knew you'd be protected." This gave people the confidence to speak up and go out on a limb, when necessary, to problem solve. As the company began to hire outside specialists, however, Smith and his colleagues felt increasingly adrift. Over time, their division lost that pack-like sense of loyalty and trust. "One day we looked around and realized that the firm had become an association of strangers," he said.

The antidote to this is a strong corporate culture that puts a premium on its workers' well-being and happiness. Research shows that trust and friendships on the job play an important role in a company's success, while an increase in morale results in a corresponding increase in the bottom line. A recent study by Hewitt Associates found that companies with high employee engagement outperformed the total stock market index and posted shareholder returns 19 percent above average for the Dow Jones in 2009. In contrast, companies with low employee engagement posted returns 44 percent below average. You can create a friendly workplace simply by following a few basic rules.

Rule 1: Look for a Doglike Friendliness

One of the easiest ways to keep that pack-like feeling is to hire folks with doglike personalities. The Kaplan Thaler Group—one of the nation's fastest-growing ad agencies—hires people with a doglike enthusiasm "because they are friendlier, they work well with the clients, have high energy, and are generally more productive," Robin Koval, the company's president, told me in an interview. She said that she watches to see how each job candidate "sniffs people out" and relates to the secretaries and receptionists. "Everybody is smart enough to be nice to the boss," she said, "but we're looking for people who play well with others. We're a service organization, and our livelihood depends on our ability to create good relationships with clients. If my people don't treat the junior product manager well, the tension in the room can undermine that." In short, there's no jockeying for power in her pack.

Rule 2: Cultivate a Doglike Empathy

Dogs are always looking out for one another and constantly provide their peers with important feedback. "To have a cohesive team," Koval said, "you have to do the same. We don't want to be like those big cold corporations that insist on formality in the workplace. We want our staff to talk about what they do outside the office, what movies they enjoy, what trips they take. These are the things that make us who we are. In advertising, our passionate likes and dislikes are important. They help us to empathize with others and understand the different segments of our audience."

Koval unabashedly takes inspiration from her dog, a black standard poodle named Ella. "What makes her such a good companion is the way she keys into my facial expression and watches me so attentively," she said. "She always responds to my moods. Dogs are incredibly empathetic. This is how we try to approach our clients."

Koval recently summoned that doglike empathy. When asked to create an ad for Trojan condoms, she called a team meeting to talk about the vagaries of the dating world. Encouraged by Koval to share jokes and personal experiences, the team developed an award-winning television spot. A beautiful girl walks into a bar and is approached by a hairy pig. In the background, we hear a plaintive song:

I ask you for your number, I ask you for a dance,
But no matter what I say, I see the question in your eyes …

The pig goes to the men's room and puts a few coins in the condom dispenser. By the time he makes it back to the bar, he has turned into an attractive guy.

This modern fairy tale with a twist makes us laugh at stereotypes (the commercial indicates that real men are "evolved" and sensitive) and provides important information about preventing STDs. This doglike empathy is highly valued at the Palo Alto, California, design firm IDEO as well. According to an article in *Fast Company* magazine, this award-winning firm has produced everything from a needle-free vaccine to a new system for airport security because its engineers have a knack for doing research into consumer needs. For example, one wore a video camera on a visit to the emergency room to document what it feels like to be left alone on a gurney. Another had his chest waxed to understand the pain that patients often experience as their surgical bandages are removed. These experiments led to the design of a more compassionate ER and a better bandage.

IDEO's designers deliberately handicap themselves to create products for special audiences. That's similar to the kind of altruistic behavior that I've noticed in dogs. Big dogs routinely handicap themselves when they play with little dogs, readily adjusting their point of view to take different sizes and strengths into account. This turns out to be a powerful principle in the business world as well.

David Kelley, chairman and founder of IDEO, made a name for himself by creating the "lavatory occupied" sign for the airline industry. But instead of staying at the large design firm he was then working at, he instead chose to work with a group of friends. His goal was to keep the focus on the personal. At IDEO people are encouraged to solve problems from the inside out, not from some theoretical remove. They put themselves in the consumer's place, asking, "What do people really need?" and "How do we make their world a better place?" This philosophy has bought the firm to national prominence. IDEO now holds more than 1,000 patents and has received 350 design awards.

RULE 3: TAKE A CANINE APPROACH TO CUSTOMER RELATIONS

There's a wonderful cartoon of a dog in a suit, looking at his boss. "I take time to lick the customer's face," he says. "I wag my tail when they talk. I jump up and down when they walk through the door. That's what sets me apart from all the other salesmen!"

Tony Hsieh's success at Zappos is closely linked to his notion that he's not in the business of selling shoes, but of "delivering happiness." He's not a fashionista. He's a former techie who's probably worn the same pair of beat-up sneakers for the last twenty years. What he cares about is creating unforgettable service and making a positive connection with his customers.

As he recounts in *Delivering Happiness: A Path to Profits, Passion, and Purpose*, Hsieh hired the world's most upbeat people to work at his call centers. Then he told them to take as long as they needed with each customer, and to be as friendly as possible. Determined to prove that his workforce was the most responsive, Hsieh once asked a colleague to call his customer service line from his hotel room in Las Vegas to ask if she could get a pizza delivered to her door at 10 P.M. Although the request had nothing to do with any of the company's products, the Zappos employee called back within five minutes with the names of three local pizza parlors in a twenty-block radius. As Hsieh says, his goal isn't just to make a sale. It's to build a relationship. That's how you get a customer for life.

The Ritz-Carlton shows the same loyalty to its up-scale guests, authorizing its employees to spend up to $2,000 a day per guest to respond to special requests and ensure a memorable stay. These resorts have managed to keep their brand intact and stay profitable, despite being taken over by budget-conscious Marriott. When guests arrive at a Ritz-Carlton, they know they'll be treated like royalty.

What the employees at these two very different companies have in common is a doglike devotion and willingness to please.

RULE 4: FORGIVE YOUR CLIENTS

I keep a cartoon on my desk showing a mutt who's torn apart a shoe and left a puddle in the middle of the floor. The caption: "Your dog knows that no matter what he does, you're going to forgive him." And I've scribbled a note beneath for the benefit of my staff that says: "That's how we ought to treat our member companies, as well."

My organization, the American Pet Products Association, represents manufacturers in the United States and abroad. Our Global Pet Expo attracts more than 10,000 visitors, and during setup we sometimes have some stressful moments. On the floor of this annual trade show, there's always a bit of jockeying for the best display booth and the most attention. Last year in Florida, the makers of some high-end dog outfits were having a rough day. First, they said the exhibit hall was too hot. Then it was too cold. Then they complained that their booth was in a bad location. Finally, they told our floor rep that the display of canned dog food right next to them had a "disturbing smell." At this point, our rep was ready to go on the defensive. We'd all worked hard to put this show together, and no other exhibitor seemed to have so many problems. I told our rep that the best thing she could do was listen to these folks, and nod sympathetically, since people often need to vent. She then made some adjustments to the thermostat and repositionied the product in their booth. Our exhibitors calmed down as soon as they realized we were acting in good faith.

Whenever there's a stressful encounter, big dogs are generally the most gracious. Because they have size in their favor, they are usually the first to back down. They also have a wide range of diplomatic skills. Most dogs value the harmony in the pack much more than a show of dominance. When one dog is trying to make friends with another, he will often take a submissive posture: lowered head, soft voice, tail down, and flash a conciliatory grin (yes, dogs can set their mouths into a smile). When you're running a service organization, as I do, it helps to master these skills.

A few years ago, an Italian CEO waited until the last minute to ship his product to our trade show in the United States. On opening day, he stood there staring at an empty exhibition booth, growing more and more irate. He didn't speak English, so we called Gina, the APPA's general counsel at the time, to translate. By the time she arrived, the CEO was demanding that we call the head of the Transportation Security Administration and the Secretary of State. Clearly, he felt we had to do something to help him get his samples out of customs! We contacted an international shipping firm that we regularly use to transport pet products. Using their contact at the airport, we were able to get the CEO's shipment delivered to the conference area.

While it wasn't my first instinct, I deferred to this man to keep the peace, because that's what any self-respecting big dog would do. I understood that this CEO was behaving aggressively because he found himself in unfamiliar territory, so I did everything I could to put him at ease. After we got his product delivered, we also placed signs at the front gate directing people to his booth and gave him "pride of place." The CEO was thrilled and the day ended well for both of us.

I reminded my staff to follow the example of big dogs: be generous with others and avoid confrontation whenever possible.

Rule 5: Forgive Your Staff

A dog never falters in his devotion to us—no matter how badly we disappoint him. As a variation on the old proverb goes, "To err is human, to forgive canine."

There are times, of course, when you need to extend forgiveness to your staff as well as your clients. The fact is we learn through our mistakes, and every good leader has to master the art of turning an ordinary gaffe into a "teaching moment."

When we got back from the trade show that year, I took my staff to a local restaurant and held a contest for the "Biggest Screw Up." I led off, telling the story of the Italian CEO, and noted that we could avoid such problems in the future by sending our international members a list of shipping companies that could deliver their products on time. Then I asked the others to share their stories. Someone pointed out that we had botched the registration process. We'd mailed badges to our early sign-ups so they could skip the registration line. But we'd forgotten to include their plastic badge holders. We also talked about another show that had set up an area for performing dogs, thinking this would be an entertaining addition to our Expo. But someone pointed out that when the dogs jumped into the air to catch a Frisbee, they landed in a pool of water, splashing the exhibitors in a nearby booth. Clearly, they hadn't thought about what playful dogs might do! This was a mistake we were able to head off at the pass. The next year we decided to have a canine fashion show, where the dogs' performance would be confined to a runway. In this informal meeting, we had some good laughs and got the information we needed to do things better. The "Biggest Screw Up" contest is now an annual tradition.

RULE 6: KNOW YOUR ROLE IN THE PACK

If you've ever seen *Dog Whisperer with Cesar Millan* on television, you've heard his advice for getting your pack to behave: assert your role as the alpha dog. This makes sense if, like Millan, you are dealing with a group of strange dogs that weren't raised together as a pack and are therefore competing for position. These twenty dogs had no knowledge of each other's skills or temperaments, so Millan had to adopt a "command-and-control" approach to bring them in line. That's the same approach many CEOs take when presiding over large organizations. Their employees, like Millan's group of dogs, have been thrown together randomly. They aren't used to each other and need to be taught how to work toward a common goal.

When companies grow beyond a certain size, the leader may feel like he's managing a bunch of strays. The goal is to draw them together and build strong working relationships. A natural dog pack is made up of family members. Because these animals have been raised together, they can easily read each other's reactions. They rely on each other's strengths and on lifelong bonds of loyalty and trust. The pack is both egalitarian and spontaneous. These dogs also provide each other with continual feedback, so there's no need for an alpha dog to wield control. This is the hallmark of a strong company as well: it can run without a leader, because it draws on its cohesiveness and on the pack's collective intelligence.

Rule 7: Think with Your Heart

Most of us are drilled to think first about the bottom line. But if we started to think like a dog, we'd focus all the time on pleasing others.

Each time we start a project, I remind my team that our solutions always need to be about relationships. "Don't just think in terms of numbers," I advise them. "Think about the effect your ideas are going to have *on people*."

At APPA, everyone has a voice in strategic planning and problem solving. My managers help define our focus for the coming year and determine the spirit in which our work gets done. Our core value has always been collaboration and teamwork.

In the dog pack, all decisions are made for the common good. That means always being aware of the effect your actions and decisions have on others. Sigal Barsade, a management professor at the

Wharton School of the University of Pennsylvania, says this is also the best way to avoid employee burnout—people generally lose heart not because the work is overwhelming but because they don't feel valued and respected on the job. In other words, you shouldn't be focused on serving only your clients; you should also be serving each other. Recently we've read a lot about the "selfish" gene. But the truth is that most of us are hardwired to cooperate and reach out to others. The brain produces more endorphins and other "feel-good" chemicals when we act in partnership with others. That's why, when nurturing and training employees, we should aim for group cohesiveness. So what are some of the best ways to achieve this?

Chapter 4

Cultivate a Canine Sense of Play

D ogs are never afraid to look foolish; they provide endless entertainment, and can turn the world's worst blooper, like snatching a pot roast from the table, into a "bonding" moment. Business leaders can benefit from their example by being willing to appear vulnerable and sometimes even a little foolish in front of the staff.

As a young engineer, I was put in charge of a department at Union Carbide and took my responsibilities, and myself, a bit too seriously. I'd come in and give people a curt nod, acting as if I knew their jobs. But I had a lot to learn. The department made a vinyl film for packaging, and I had no idea that, as it went through the production line, it built up a strong static charge. One day the machine jammed and the operators asked me to help fix it. You could hear the guffaws as I leaned over the equipment and my hair stood on end. At this point I stopped pretending I knew what I was doing. And as I joined the laughter, I realized I'd passed a test.

From that moment on, people were more at ease with me. When they discovered that I had a sense of humor, they began to stop by my office toward the end of the day. They'd tell a joke or two, and, in the process, alert me to any problems on the production line. At the same time, they felt free to ask for help, knowing I wouldn't judge them for their failures or lord it over them for days to come. Humor, I discovered, is a leveling factor. So my advice is to find an appropriate time to shed your authority and acknowledge that, as a manager, you are both flawed and human.

When a dog plays, he rolls over and bares his most vulnerable parts—his neck and belly—to show that he has absolute faith and trust in his companion. Managers need to show their vulnerability as well. The best of all leaders, Tony Schwartz wrote in a blog on the website of the *Harvard Business Review*, are those who have the capacity to embrace vulnerability alongside strength and humility alongside confidence. "Great leaders don't feel the need to be right, or to be perfect," he noted, "because they've learned to value themselves in spite of their shortcomings which they freely acknowledge. In turn, they bring this generous spirit to those they lead."

By accepting your own imperfections, you give other people the right to make mistakes. Your subordinates will spend more time on the job, and less time defending themselves and rationalizing their choices, because they fear being called on the carpet or criticized. They will also be more innovative, for their first concern will no longer be to hide behind the rules and "play it safe."

If you have the courage to embrace your vulnerability, you can change the tone of the entire workplace. It's no longer about hierarchy and who reports to whom. It's about being part of a team that values all people equally and shares triumphs as well as mistakes.

You can build rapport with your staff and show that you have a sense of humor by injecting some canine craziness into your workday. Tell a story about yourself at a meeting or during lunch to show how little you once knew about a company's product or procedures. Encourage others to share their most hilarious mistakes and use humor to teach. Keep cartoons on your desk or put up a joke board.

When a Manhattan bank was training bank tellers, they found that nearly everyone made the same simple errors. Supervisors pointed out the problem, but the tellers continued to make the same mistakes. Finally, the company put up a series of funny posters showing how easy it was for anyone to goof up. The tellers cracked up when they saw this lampoon of "common screw-ups," and their performance steadily improved. Humor helps to cement information in our brains at the same times it improves our mood.

A dog will never pass up an opportunity to amuse: if he can make you laugh, he knows he's done his job. Laughter and a sense of play do a lot more than relieve the daily grind—they ultimately build trust, acceptance, and stronger relationships.

RULE 1: PUT SOME FUN INTO YOUR FIRM

If you honor your canine wisdom, you'll create a company that looks more like a playground than an inverted pyramid.

"Fun is one of the important aspects of working here," Niki Leondakis, COO of Kimpton Hotels & Restaurants, told *The New York Times*. "For a leader, the ability to laugh at yourself is key, so we use Hula-Hoops to demonstrate that." Kimpton holds a "hoop off" at the company's annual meeting. The new managers come up to the front of the room and start "hooping" to the tune of *Wipe Out*. The winner then goes up against last year's reigning champion. The idea is for people to become comfortable doing new things and taking risks in front of each other.

If you find this frivolous, take note: stress is one of the main causes of illness, absenteeism, and employee burnout, according to clinical psychologist Steven Sultanoff. It can disrupt key working relationships and reduce productivity. And suddenly you find your company with a severe case of the "blahs."

Humor, on the other hand, has a positive effect on morale. David Abramis reported in *HR Magazine* that individuals who feel free to express their sense of humor at the office have better mental health and more job satisfaction, and are more likely to stay at their jobs. Many compare their work to doing a puzzle or playing sports. What's more, they are more likely to have jobs that offer challenge, autonomy, variety, feedback, and a greater sense of completion.

A doglike sense of play can impact your bottom line as well. Research into creativity shows that people get their best ideas when they're not focusing on a specific problem, but are instead relaxed or engaged in some form of sport or game. According to a study by American Express, over one-third of people who worked for small businesses got their best ideas "off the job" when they were engaged in leisure activities. So perhaps it's time to reconsider "break time" and realize that folks can actually get that "big idea" when they're not at their desks. A *U.S. News & World Report* article noted that play is necessary for rejuvenation: "All Work and No Play Makes a Company... Unproductive."

RULE 2: BUILD A COMPANY "DOG RUN"

For both humans and dogs, the need to play has the same function: we develop specific skills through play that help us bond with others, survive in the world, and think outside the box. You can encourage this ease and playfulness by creating the corporate equivalent of a "dog run."

If you go to a dog park, you'll learn about the art of making friends and building new alliances. When a dog wags his tail, crouches down, and looks up at you with a half smile on his face, this is an invitation to become a trusted member of his social circle. This preliminary greeting is followed by more sophisticated interaction—chasing, tugging, wrestling, and canine hide-and-seek—during which dogs reveal their agendas.

Games also provide an opportunity for employees to get a sense of what motivates themselves and their coworkers. Companies have traditionally used sports teams and company retreats to foster a canine sense of playfulness and camaraderie. The rationale is simple: if you can roll in the dirt with your colleagues, then you're considered part of the pack.

If I want to understand how my colleagues will react in a difficult situation, I'll take them to the golf course and watch how they handle the challenges of a bad shot or getting out of a sand trap. Similarly, if I want to find out if a new hire has a sense of humor, I'll invite the person to my home on a Sunday, to watch a Giants football game with my dog, Dakota, and me, followed by a game of fetch on the back lawn.

These unguarded moments can provide valuable insights into how people perform under pressure and where they find the most joy.

In a contracting economy, employee morale goes down due to belt-tightening. The cheapest and easiest way to address that is to add a bit of fun and camaraderie to the workplace. Here's why.

RULE 3: LAUGHTER LEADS TO COLLABORATION

Humor is an important element of a corporate culture because it carries a message of equality: I will treat you with kindness. I will not try to dominate. If you look at any photo of your family dog, you'll see that he's a master at giving these cues.

Warm, openhearted laughter is a cue that we are not a threat to others. This activity turns off the fight-or-flight response and reduces adrenaline. It not only relaxes people, but it also gets us in sync with other people and enhances creativity.

Bring your sense of humor to work every day. Show your staff that you don't take yourself or the title above your door too seriously. Don't limit the use of humor to what's politically correct—doing so can lead to rigidity and stuffiness, the two things that are guaranteed to snuff out creativity. Instead, begin to understand what your staff finds funny. Humor is personal: if you get to know your staff, you'll know what kind of jokes are appropriate to lighten up their days.

I'll never forget the manufacturing executive who fell off the stage while receiving a trophy for the "best performance" in her division. She didn't miss a beat. She just waved her hand and said, "And now I'd like to make a few comments from the floor." Humor like this shows strength of character and resilience. And it also allows you to model "grace under fire."

You can't control how people will respond in a crisis, but you can prepare them to meet it with good humor.

RULE 4: TURN PLAY INTO PROFITS

A doglike sense of play can help you to increase productivity. As I've said, a dog will try to solve a problem, as long as the activity feels like fun. But the moment it gets boring, he disengages. People are the same; when their work starts to slide, you can bet that at least part of the problem is that they're stuck in a mind-numbing routine and are desperate for some stimulation and variety.

There are a number of reasons employees become disaffected. But boredom ranks up at the top, according to a 2010 survey by Robert Half International, a recruiting firm. One out of every five Americans finds work to be repetitive or dull. In a tight economy, people are also worried and anxious. Many are so concerned about keeping their jobs that they have a hard time concentrating on the work at hand. My advice to all types of managers: if you want to engage your workers, lighten up.

Firms in Silicon Valley were among the first to create the perfect corporate kennel, providing gourmet cafeterias, exercise rooms, and games, to give employees a few hours off the leash. Google has a foosball machine and snacks in the break room, Adobe has an outdoor basketball court, and many companies have high-tech gyms. The Palo Alto design company IDEO holds its idea meetings in a brightly painted Volkswagen bus.

The companies named by *Entrepreneur* magazine as the best small and medium companies to work for value games, activities, and bonding rituals:

- AMX, a technology company in Richardson, Texas, encourages people to "work barefoot, listen to rock and roll, or play jokes on their coworkers," while keeping their performance at the highest levels.

- Ehrhardt Keefe Steiner & Hottman, an accounting firm in Denver, Colorado, gives out a Standing on Your Head award, which comes with a dinner at an upscale restaurant and a limo.

- Root Learning, a strategic consulting firm in Sylvania, Ohio, helps students to create Learning Maps to envision their future. They also post a portrait of new hires, mapping their hobbies and personal interests on a "family tree" in the front lobby.

- Johnson & Johnson, Inc., a family-owned financial services and insurance company in Charleston, South Carolina, sponsors ugly sweater competitions and chili cook-offs to forge a strong bond among employees.

- Insomniac Games, a game developer in Burbank, California, holds regular "show-and-tells" to showcase the latest video games, and every Friday hosts late-night gaming sessions.

- Professional Placement Resources, a staffing agency in Jacksonville Beach, Florida, brings people together with scavenger hunts and electronic bingo.

America's best places to work are also among the most creative. They provide variety, physical stimulation, and games that hone our mental faculties. And the results are improved morale, increased productivity, and greater passion and commitment.

Rule 5: Know Your Pack

Just like you have to be sure that the dog toys you choose are safe, you also need to make sure the type of play you offer corresponds to the needs and values of your pack.

Collies need to herd, pointers need to hunt, and terriers need to dig until they reach the center of the earth. Know what kind of breed you're dealing with and you'll be able to choose those activities that are most likely to appeal to them. Take what happened when the Phelps Group, a marketing and communications firm in Santa Monica, California, booked a ranch in Malibu for a company retreat. They set up teepees on the beach, dressed their CEO in a Native American headdress and full war paint, and propelled him down the beach in an all-terrain vehicle. Then the ATV carrying the CEO hit a rock and overturned. By the time their leader made it to the tent, his stance was wobbly and his headdress resembled a dead parrot. Meanwhile, the employees had no idea what ritual was being enacted. Displays like this can leave employees with a sense of unease.

Cynthia McKay, CEO of Le Gourmet Gift Basket, learned that there are pitfalls in using sports as a bonding agent when she took the staff of her Evanston, Illinois-based company to a ski resort in Vail, Colorado. One employee fell and broke her leg, another fractured her arm, and a third employee ran into a tree. Others pulled tendons. A postmortem on the trip revealed that her employees considered themselves "indoor people" and would rather play the slots in Las Vegas.

Today companies are turning to indoor play-ground coordinators like Pump It Up that provide safe "team-building" events that use obstacle courses, inflatable slides, and scavenger hunts. There's enough variety for the physically active and for the average couch potato. "It's a break for us," Lucy Rermgosakul, of TEKsystems, an information-technology staffing firm in Hanover, Maryland, told *The Baltimore Sun*. "It's a fun way to show how we can cooperate with one another when faced with difficult challenges. And it opens up different ways of communication for people who are shyer."

If play seems like an optional perk, consider this: Americans are more prone to feel overworked than their European counterparts, and more likely to experience burnout. One in four American work-ers has no paid vacation, and nearly half fail to take as much as a week off every year, according to *U.S. News & World Report*. In addition, the average em-ployee now works more than thirty days more per year than she did in 1976.

This brings us to the most pressing question for any corporate leader today: how can you innovate—

and keep creating new products and new technologies—if your people are dog tired and can't stay up to speed?

Chapter 5

Foster Dogged Innovation

I nnovation is the lifeblood of any company, so you're in serious danger when it starts to ebb. When I was a director at First Brands, we were losing market share for one of our bestselling products. Our R&D group wasn't coming up with new ideas fast enough. We'd also lost a few of our veterans, and the newcomers were afraid to speak up and take a risk. Given this sensitive situation, I couldn't point to another, more successful division of the company and say, "Why don't you try this team's approach?" If I had, my people would have totally shut down.

I needed a nonthreatening way to get them going, so I began to talk about my dog and the way he problem-solves. That weekend, Samson had tried for hours to get a tennis ball out from under a van. First, he attempted to nudge it with his nose. Then he batted it with his paw. When he discovered it was too far to reach, he scrunched his body under the van until his hips got caught on the undercarriage and he couldn't go any farther. It took him another fifteen minutes to work his way back out. Then, inspiration struck. The neighborhood cat, a black-and-white tabby, had been watching from her usual place by our white picket fence. Samson managed to sneak up behind the cat then chased it under the van, successfully using it as a cue ball. As the cat whizzed by, she hit the tennis ball and seconds later, Samson had it in his possession. He spent the rest of the afternoon methodically gnawing at it.

This story got a lot of laughs and made my point effectively: you have to be willing to try a lot of solutions that might seem ridiculous before you land on one that works.

At our next concept meeting, I urged my designers and engineers to take a similarly dogged approach to upgrading one of our best-known products, GLAD bags. The division president, George Vestal, sat in on our idea session and asked, "Is this the guy who tells stories about his dog? How's he going to teach our people about creativity?" I grinned and explained that I was going to invoke dogs yet again to get us all into a different mind-set.

First, I put a pile of GLAD bags on the table and asked my team to act like dogs going after a bone and rip the product apart. I urged them to attack it from every conceivable angle, and then to give me a list of its weaknesses and flaws.

It took a few minutes for everyone to get into the swing of it, but once the senior managers joined in and, more importantly, refrained from making negative comments, we had a productive meeting. At one point, a junior engineer took out his lunch, a tuna sandwich wrapped in a GLAD bag, to show us that the fold-over top didn't have a strong enough seal. The package leaked as soon as he turned it upside down, so we came up with about ten ridiculous ideas on how to fix it. One possibility was to use Velcro or apply some kind of sticky strips to keep it shut (which would, of course, make it hard to open again). Another was to create a bag shaped like a bottle, with a wide mouth. While we were trying to make one of these crazy ideas work, an engineer returned from the men's room with his shirt stuck in his fly. Someone quipped that since zippers grabbed so well we should put a zipper on the bag. Bingo!! We quickly made a prototype and Vestal scheduled a sales call with a big retailer to show off the world's first bag with a zip closure. We had yet to build the machine to manufacture it, so Vestal went into the meeting with a handmade sample. Before we could stop him, he poured his coffee into the bag and then tossed it into the buyer's lap. We all held our breath since we'd never tried that. Thankfully, the seal held and we walked away with a huge order.

The moral of the story is that true innovation begins with dogged perseverance and a willingness to bend the rules.

At Stanford University's Graduate School of Business, Michael Ray has spent the past twenty years teaching future MBAs how to problem solve. His marketing course is legendary, and in the past decade, Ray has taught students who've gone on to become top executives at Charles Schwab, Hewlett Packard, and Clorox. Ray gets people down on the floor to color with crayons, draw in journals, meditate, and do team-building exercises. I've learned a lot from Ray and other creativity experts. At the

American Pet Products Association, we have Magic Markers at every concept meeting, and I encourage everyone to doodle. The idea is to occupy the conscious brain with some simple task, and free the subconscious part to experiment. Staff members often sit there playing tic-tac-toe or drawing a caricature of me, their erstwhile boss. But it's in these freewheeling moments that the mind spins into a new orbit and we get our most useful ideas.

The message I give my staff during this warm-up exercise is to try anything once. Don't be afraid to look foolish. Take risks. And don't second-guess yourself.

Self-consciousness is a peculiarly human trait that stops us cold and keeps us from tapping into our full potential. Since the US economy depends on the generation of new products and ideas, no CEO can afford to ignore this message or write it off as "frivolous."

Rule 1: Go for Quantity, Not Quality

Animal trainers will tell you that the quickest way to break a dog's spirit is to repeatedly tell him what he can't do. Similarly, the greatest enemy of creativity is the voice that says, "It can't be done."

When I want to get new ideas from my staff, I make sure they know that what I care about is the free flow of ideas, not about whether they're feasible. No one is allowed to shoot a concept down because we never know which seemingly wrongheaded notion will suddenly transform into a workable one.

Bob Moog, president of University Games, an educational game developer in San Francisco, California, told *Fast Company* magazine that when faced with a design problem, the most valuable thing you can do is to ignore your knee-jerk assumptions and generate alternative scenarios. "Successful people tend to [rely] on past experiences in similar situations," he said. "But we live in a world where things are changing so fast that if you rely on what you knew five years ago, you're not going to come up with the best answer."

Moog gives his designers some counterintuitive advice: Don't try to be efficient. Slow down and explore the options. New ideas are better than recycled solutions. To take a dogged approach to innovation, you have to be willing to go past the tried and true.

Rule 2: Keep Your Creative Teams Small

Dog packs function fluidly and flawlessly because these groups are small, usually consisting of five to eight members. There's no need for an alpha dog because everyone is related. Members know how to read each other's most subtle cues and exchange roles and responsibilities as needed. That's how good creative teams operate as well.

The American Pet Products Association runs on this model. Our marketing, membership, trade show, finance, and administrative support departments are all operated by pack-sized teams. The result is a "family feeling" where everyone feels supported. This helps us to take risks and explore the limits of our imagination. A survey of our trade show exhibitors indicates that APPA members create somewhere between 3,500 and 4,000 new products every year—a strong track record for innovation.

The business leaders I've interviewed for this book note that the dog pack is a good model for most steering committees and management teams as well—things work smoothly when a few individuals work toward a common goal, then report back to the CEO.

"If the group is larger, it's too easy to disagree and get into heated discussions," W. Stanton Smith said. "When you have more people, it's hard to give everyone a chance to speak, and if you do, you risk slowing things down. You can't run a business when anybody can throw sand in the gears at any time."

In the digital age, "pack-size" turns out to be ideal for virtual teams as well.

"Go beyond seven people and you just have too many to communicate with online," Bill Scudder, vice president and chief information officer at Sonus Networks, a computer networking provider in Westford, Massachusetts, said in an interview. "If you've only got an hour for a videoconference, you have to keep it tight," Scudder advised. "You can't manage time effectively if the group is too large. And if it's too small, you don't cover all the bases."

Entrepreneur Fred Seddiqui agreed. "I keep my management teams down to seven," he said. "Beyond that, there is too much opportunity for debate. If you keep your committees and your management team lean, it's easier to move ahead quickly."

"Pack-size" is as important for established companies as it is for high-tech start-ups. Researchers have also found that the smaller the team, the less propensity there is for "social loafing" or letting other people do the work. A study published in the *Journal of Management Information Systems* shows that as team size increases members have less of a stake in the outcome and tend to make fewer contributions.

The "pack principle" applies on Madison Avenue as well. Ad agencies usually team up a writer and an art director, and then ask them to pitch their concept. "One of the things that makes Kaplan Thaler different," Robin Koval said, "is that we bring in a team of six or eight together and let them pitch to one another. We get better results when we function like a sled dog team."

No one has embraced the pack mentality more than Generation Y. "They have a tendency to work in packs because they've been doing so since grade school—on both Internet projects and sports teams. And they dislike hierarchy because they grew up in egalitarian households and were always questioning their teachers," Donna Fenn, author of *Upstarts! How GenY Entrepreneurs Are Rocking the World of Business and 8 Ways You Can Profit from Their Success*, told me.

Fenn was surprised to find that more people in their twenties are starting their own businesses than ever before. "A lot of them were in the tech space, but not all," Fenn said. "So I began to wonder, 'What kind of companies are they building? Are they different from the ones we've seen in the past?'"

The answer is yes. For one thing, this generation really likes to work in collaborative packs. They also tend to hire their friends. Fenn recounted how Nick

Friedman and Omar Soliman, who met in the tenth grade, later founded College Hunks Hauling Junk, a service based in Tampa, Florida, that picks up unwanted items and recycles most of them. They've turned their pack model into a national franchise, with operations in twenty-six cities.

Born between 1979 and 1995, members of Generation Y are pack-like in other ways. They tend to stay in touch with the pack outside of the office, too, and freely socialize with their coworkers. There are now over 77 million of them, and "they are happiest when their work and life are a mash-up," Fenn said. "Gen Yers are more ecological: they take their operating model from nature, and prefer to work with family and friends," she added.

What's more, women prefer to work in tight-knit packs because it affords them a chance to get to know each other and be more emotionally engaged. Researchers at Carnegie Mellon University, MIT, and Union College found that this is a plus because the collective intelligence of a team is higher when the individuals are more intimate or socially attuned. After studying 700 people who worked in groups, scientists reported that the more women you put on your team, the more you expand your skills. This isn't just about brainpower. It's about social skills, and knowing how to get the best from others. My office is 80 percent female, and I agree with the researchers' observations that women tend to cooperate, rather than vie for power, while sharing information and resources.

If you want to create more effective teams, my advice is to add more women. If you can't change the gender balance, make sure your people get more face time.

Rule 3: Do Something Unexpected

Dogs are wonderfully spontaneous and are constantly improvising in order to get our attention. This ability can help you with your customers as well. When Bob Moog founded University Games, he suddenly found himself up against the toy industry giants Hasbro and Mattel. At first, buyers weren't even returning his sales calls, so Moog came up with an amusing strategy to capture their attention, which he explained to *Fast Company* magazine. Since he was marketing a Batman game, he made up a batch of door signs showing Gotham's superhero with the caption: "Do not disturb me. I'm out saving the world." On the flip side, he put the Joker with the caption, "Diabolical Plot in Progress. Come on in."

"A lot of the buyers put the tags right on their doors," Moog said. "We'd call their assistants and ask, 'What side is showing?' Whenever it was the Joker, we were put right through."

This brings us back to the lesson in our previous chapter: a good joke makes any message go down easier. Year after year, the ads that win the most awards are by far the funniest. No matter what product you make or market, you need to create a climate where people are playful and free to innovate.

Using humor gives us an opportunity to do the unexpected. It also reduces stress and increases endorphins and other "feel-good" chemicals in the brain. This is why games are so addictive—they provide us with a physical high. So remember, when you surprise someone, the amygdala—or the portion of the brain that processes emotions—lights up. And the experience is more memorable.

RULE 4: DO WHAT YOU LOVE

Both dogs and human beings evolve by doing what they love. Inventions don't grow out of a blueprint. They come from hours of joyful play and experimentation. For example, the company now called Facebook was launched from a Harvard dorm room when Mark Zuckerberg, along with cofounders Dustin Moskovitz, Chris Hughes, and Eduardo Saverin, discovered a new way of socializing. They built the site for the thrill of creating something new, just as hundreds of techies had cobbled together the Internet a few decades before.

So how do you get your people into this frame of mind? Awaken their childlike innocence and remind them that there are endless possibilities.

I recommend you start a meeting with a few playful exercises. First, give people what's known as the "Purdue Intelligence Test": take three minutes to come up with as many novel uses as possible for a paper clip. (This is the equivalent of throwing a tennis ball under a van and watching your dog come up with ten different ways to get at it, as it requires the ability to visualize new uses for common things and encourages experimentation.) Then ask them to share their results.

Next, try the circle test—this is a favorite at the design firm IDEO. Ask how many things your colleagues can make out of thirty circles. Show them a few examples: a Christmas ornament, a compass, a model of the planet Saturn. Then give them two sheets of paper, with the outline of fifteen circles drawn on each, and let them have a go at it. The person with the most ideas wins—and make sure they get points if they "steal" or incorporate your examples. Remember, most good ideas build on earlier inventions. You're also going for sheer volume, not checking to see if you're about to violate somebody's copyright.

Rule 5: Think Outside the Cubicle

The most innovative CEOs today embrace everything from the downright wacky to the irreverent. Procter & Gamble even invited people from other companies and other walks of life to contribute product ideas to their "idea box." Eastman Kodak learned that creativity blossoms in an atmosphere of looseness and informality when it allowed engineers to experiment with new designs right on the walls of its skunkworks in Rochester, New York. Working "in grunge" is a way of saying, "We're not playing by the rules." Silicon Valley gets this, too. When Google first opened its doors, people came to work barefoot, in cutoffs, and in jeans. At APPA, we have a business casual dress code Monday through Thursday. Friday is Come as You Are Day and we occasionally go off-site, holding meetings at a local Italian restaurant. Wine, I've found, is an excellent lubricant for creativity and candor.

Dogs need the stimulation of new sights, sounds, and smells to develop their brains. For people to stay sharp, they need a varied work environment. In 2010, *Inc.* magazine's website teamed up with Architizer, an online community for architects, to identify "cool office spaces," casual work areas that are likely to enhance innovation. You find lockers and fabric storage bins on wheels at Vitra, a furniture company based in Birsfelden, Switzerland, stacked lacquered boxes that serve as mini-studios at Pallotta TeamWorks, an event-planning company in Los Angeles, and meeting rooms with comfy couches at Big River, an advertising agency in Richmond, Virginia. I give first prize to IPEVO, a product design firm with offices in Sunnyvale, California, and Taipei, Taiwan. The firm's Taipei office embraces the outdoors with a virtual dog run with trees, plants, and grass floors. This area also functions as a reception area and place for employees to hang out.

Chapter 6

Bring Fido to Work

One way to create an atmosphere that's more relaxed, playful, and productive is to allow employees to bring their pets to work. According to an American Pet Products Association survey, one in five companies now encourage their staff to do this, whether it's for a trial run or the entire year.

For the past decade, we've been supporting Take Your Dog to Work Day, a program started by Pet Sitters International. Google, Amazon, and software developer AutoDesk were among the first places to bring their dogs to the office since employees were working 24/7 and didn't have time to go home to feed their pets. Since then, researchers have discovered a host of other benefits. As Liz Palika and Jennifer Fearing pointed out in *Dogs at Work: A Practical Guide to Creating Dog-Friendly Workplaces*, many people live two lives. At home they show their true selves, but at work, they put on a mask and behave in a completely different way. At the office, they may be more competitive, authoritarian, ruthless, or ambitious. They might also be so focused on managing deadlines and meeting the boss's expectations that they forget to show their personal side. But Take Your Dog to Work Day makes the workplace more sociable, and the interaction with animals encourages people to be more open and spontaneous.

"Having dogs in the workplace creates an almost magical connection," Jeanine Falcon, human resources director at Replacements, in Greensboro, North Carolina, told me. This unusual company allows dogs into its shop filled with expensive heirloom china. "It's terrific for new hires and it gets people talking," she said. "When you see a dog in the warehouse, you stop and chat with its owner. You bond over the animal, and you get to know people in all areas of the company."

Many businesses work very hard to create the kind of "family atmosphere" that other pet-friendly companies seem to create naturally.

"It's great for our employees because it lifts their mood," Falcon said. "When you're greeted with enthusiasm by the dogs, this kind of warm, friendly reception will change your whole day. And it appeals to customers as well. We allow dogs in the showroom, and tourists come by because they know this is a pet-friendly place. They enjoy seeing a Jack Russell terrier ride by in a mail cart. And when people come in to shop, one of the first things they ask is, 'Can we please see the dogs?' You can be sure we include them on every tour."

In the past two decades, animals have become increasingly important to us. Our dogs are more than pets; they're more like family members. When Jeanine Falcon's Bernese mountain dog was diagnosed with lymphoma, she knew she could count on her coworkers for support. "I was able to bring my dog to work, take her to the vet on my lunch hour, and then keep her by my side, after she had her cancer treatment," she said. "My 'work family' knew her well and they were really there for me." In addition, at Replacements, "if you lose a dog, you hear directly from the [company] president."

Dogs have played a major role at Replacements since CEO Bob Page started bringing his dachshund to work. "If I can have this kind of companionship throughout the day," he told his HR director, "why not give the same opportunity to my employees?" Soon the whole tenor of the company changed. Today more than half of the company's 450 workers take advantage of his pet-friendly policy, Falcon said.

"Nobody used to like coming to HR," Falcon added, "because their first thought was, 'I must be in trouble.' But after I brought in my dog, Zola, people found the place more welcoming. With a dog present, it's easier for them to relax, and we can enter into a productive conversation about how they're doing on the job. There's one thing we know to be true: these animals help to break down the barriers and put the staff at ease."

When dogs visit the headquarters of Sunshine Makers, based in Huntington Beach, California, it feels like "bring your kid to work day," Carol Chapin, the company's vice president of research and development, said. Having pets stop by the company, which sells environmentally safe cleaning products under the Simple Green brand, "helps to create a friendly environment, and gives a strong message: you are working for a company that has a heart.

When buyers visit, they're impressed as well. They see our menagerie and realize we are not the typical staid corporation with cubicles. We're family run and very entrepreneurial, and for us, having dogs is an extension of that."

At the American Pet Products Association, our company dogs serve as conversation starters helping newcomers to connect with their coworkers. When Michelle and Josh joined us, they were two of the more introverted people here. The animals have given them a way to get to know their office mates. A few times a day, staff members will pair up and take one of the dogs for a walk. They might talk about who they're dating or where they're going on the weekend. While tending to the dogs, employees have found it easier to get to know each other.

Create a Positive Distraction

When we're under pressure, the dogs also provide a fail-safe way to lighten up: often Bernie, Casey, Doyle, Lola, or Perseus play around our conference table. One month we had a deadline for a promotion piece. The heads of marketing and member services had both been traveling and hadn't yet met in person to agree on the purpose of a new brochure. Finally, both parties met face-to-face, and expressed their disappointment with the final layout. During this tense exchange, Perseus and Lola started chasing each other around the conference room. We wound up playing with the dogs for a few minutes, and a few minutes later, we regrouped. By then, emotions had settled and we reached a consensus quickly.

When you're dealing with counterproductive behavior, you need a distraction to help you move away from it. Our animals always provide that shift and help us find a new perspective. They seem to have a sixth sense, always materializing at the moment they're most needed.

People often ask me, "Is it wise to have a bunch of animals running loose around the office? Don't they disrupt your routine and make it hard to do business as well?" And I say, "That's exactly why we have them. They remind us to step back and not take ourselves too seriously. They add to the creative process. And when we're stuck, they shake us up so we can refocus."

It's when our usual thinking process is derailed that we make the kind of intuitive leaps that lead to discovery and innovation. We bring our dogs to the office because they *do* distract us; afterward, we move in more fruitful directions. "That's the wonderful thing about dogs," Robin Koval said. "They're wild, wacky, hairy joy. And they always do the unexpected."

Add a New Health Benefit

We began to support Take Your Dog to Work Day because the data on animals in the workplace was so overwhelmingly positive. Karen Allen, a research associate professor of neurology at the University at

Buffalo, part of the State University of New York, has found that dogs have a therapeutic effect on people in demanding occupations, enabling them to deal more easily with stress. What's more, dogs lower our blood pressure and our heart rate, and increase our levels of oxytocin and other "feel-good" chemicals. In short, they make us feel safe and happy, so we are better able to concentrate on the task at hand.

My son Josh works in APPA's marketing department and often brings his bulldog, Perseus, to the office. I find myself petting him during my most stressful calls. On the days I have to deal with a dissatisfied member or a national crisis like a recent pet food recall, Percy keeps me calm and centered.

The American Pet Products Association commissioned a survey in 2006 to explore our attitudes toward pets in the workplace. What we found was striking:

- Fifty million workers believe that having pets in the office can lead to a more creative work environment.

- Fifty-three million said that by bringing their pets to the office, they'd need to take fewer sick days.

- Forty-six million would be willing to put in longer hours if they had their pets with them during the workday.

- Thirty-seven million said that having dogs in the workplace would improve relationships between managers and employees.

Simply Hired, a job search firm, also found that two-thirds of all dog-owning job hunters would willingly take a cut in pay if they could bring their dogs to work.

A growing number of companies, noticing significant benefits from having dogs around the office, have begun to make this a permanent policy.

(I should note that most pet-friendly firms give people who are uncomfortable around dogs for any reason the right to veto having animals near their desks. It's easy enough for most companies to set up a play area that's far enough away from sensitive individuals to keep everyone content.)

I've observed several differences in dog-friendly workplaces: in general, employees tend to be more approachable, open to new ideas, and able to make intuitive leaps. They're also more respectful of diversity. In short, pet-friendly workplaces are less structured, more casual, and more collaborative.

If you can't bring your dog to work because your building has a no-pet stipulation, there are other ways to encourage canine creativity and let your employees "off the leash." Here are some ideas that might work for your organization.

Think Canine

1. Embrace a doglike sense of play, through casual dress days, with employee break rooms, joke boards, and corporate "recess" periods.

2. Don't be afraid to get personal. Our individual passions and interests shouldn't be left at home. They help us to bond with our colleagues and customers and to create a more open, fluid workplace.

3. Encourage canine creativity. Dogs tunnel under, go around, and sneak up behind. They know that creativity is a zigzag path, not a straight line. Give your staff permission to try different approaches to product design or marketing, and to come at a problem "from the side."

4. Foster canine empathy and attentiveness. Dogs are masters of observation; in a split second they can read our intentions. Keen observation will help your employees zero in on what your clients and customers are feeling, and what services they value most.

5. Give your staff the same kind of uncritical acceptance that we get from dogs. If you want to foster innovation, you'll have to learn how to silence your own critic—the part of you that wants to jump in and explain what *won't* work and why.

PART III
THE PUPPY THEORY OF MANAGEMENT

Q. How do you give feedback?
A. I have the puppy theory. When the
puppy pees on the carpet, you say something
right then because you don't say six months
later, "Remember that day, January 12th,
when you peed on the carpet?" That doesn't
make any sense. "This is what's on my mind.
This is quick feedback." And then I'm
on to the next thing.
—Yahoo! CEO CAROL BARTZ

Chapter 7

Reward in Real Time

W hen you train a puppy, you say, "Good dog!" and immediately hold out a treat. If you wait too long, you lose your chance to reinforce good behavior. This principle is important to remember when you're training employees as well. The best management advice I have to offer: don't wait for the end-of-the-year annual review. Instead hand out your treats on the spot.

Yahoo's CEO, Carol Bartz, makes a point of acknowledging her employees' accomplishments in real time, insisting that the treat should always follow the trick. Even something as simple as a "Well done!" in a staff meeting, or a few words of appreciation at the watercooler, she told *The New York Times*, count as "positive reinforcement." Bartz previously served as CEO of Autodesk, a software developer in San Rafael, California, that was one of the first companies to let employees bring their dogs to work. This decision clearly shaped its corporate culture: the dogs reinforced bonds between the workers, set a casual, friendly tone, and made it easier for people to work overtime on high-priority projects.

"Our story is a lot like Microsoft's," Kathy Clinton, Autodesk's human resources director, told me. "Our founders started out working in a garage, and when the company grew, they brought their dogs to the office. They even have named conference rooms after them." She added, "We had a very tight culture that was ahead of its time, in terms of taking care of our employees."

Bartz is just one of many executives today who subscribe, at least in part, to what I call The Puppy Theory of Management. This makes intuitive sense to anyone who has ever owned or trained a dog. It consists of five principles that will help you engage your employees and bring their performance to a whole new level:

- Reward in Real Time
- Correct Early
- Lead by Example
- Stay on Message
- Cultivate Intelligent Disobedience

I'll address these in the following chapters, but first a word on why I make this comparison. When dogs were first domesticated, about 16,000 years ago, they not only helped us hunt and alerted us to danger, but they also socialized us. Greger Larson, an archaeologist at Durham University, believes that we wouldn't have civilization without them. With their protection, we were able to settle in one place and start planting crops. Thus began the agrarian revolution.

Dogs have always been our primary partners, and I delight in the traits we have in common: a high level of emotional intelligence, a willingness to please, the ability to work hard and to take pleasure in a job done well, a high degree of loyalty and service, a strong moral sense, and an appreciation for kindness and words of praise. Anyone who has ever had a dog is aware of these sterling qualities.

Trainers have recently begun to tap into a dog's natural intelligence so the animal can perform increasingly complex tasks, not just to satisfy its hunger or need for shelter, but also for the sheer joy of doing something well.

Animal experts say this is a radical change: we've moved beyond *conditional training*, providing rewards for good behavior and punishing a dog's errors, to *operant training*, making good performance into a habit and turning excellence into its own reward.

Enlightened trainers have far more respect for the individual dog, and a greater understanding of its potential, than those who use the old-fashioned approach of "reward and reprimand." Similarly, enlightened managers now have a greater respect and understanding of what motivates their colleagues and coworkers.

RULE 1: REWARD 24/7

When one of my managers does an outstanding job, I try to respond with a "thank you" within twenty-four hours. This might be a dinner out, an extra day off, or a gift card to a local shop. Every manager needs a discretionary fund to reward employees who have gone beyond the call of duty or simply done a stellar job. This is true even in a stalled economy when budgets are tight and bonuses are shrinking.

In early 2010, general economic projections were so worrisome that our board insisted on a salary freeze. The pet industry continued to grow, and I had to find some way to reward my top people while I adhered to the new policy. That meant getting creative, such as giving them a pair of baseball tickets, a day off to volunteer for a charity, or a gift certificate to a local restaurant.

Studies show that employees may prefer these personalized gifts to token raises that don't even keep pace with the cost of living. "When you give less than 5 percent, it almost seems like a slap in the face," Mike Figliuolo, founder and managing director of *thoughtLEADERS*, a management consulting firm, told me. It's "better to give something practical that a person will be able to use and appreciate," he said. That's why retailers and food chains have started giving deeper discounts to employees.

The other practice I recommend is to "pay it forward"—pass along any compliments that come from top management or the board of directors. When our chairman was impressed by a new member service, I sent a note to my team, saying, "The credit for this belongs to you."

Finally, I try to keep it personal, mentioning that I appreciate Michelle's sunny personality and her ability to engage the public; Jenn's patience when she has to deal with difficult membership requests; or Josh's ability to crack us up with a practical joke when a meeting gets too tense.

In this age of ephemeral communication—e-mail, texting, and Twitter—it's also easy to underestimate the impact of a handwritten note. At the end of the week, Mike Figliuolo takes the time to review the contributions of his staff then dashes off a personal note to the person who did the most outstanding job. "You gave a stellar presentation," he might say. Or, "You really helped our client take their thinking to the next level." Then he leaves it on the employee's chair.

One morning, a team member came into Figliuolo's office, beaming.

"I finally did it," he said. "I finally got one!"

"Got what?" Figliuolo asked.

The employee walked Figliuolo past cubicles, pointing out the notes that Figliuolo had written, which were posted on bulletin boards or computer monitors. One was even in a frame, right next to the employee's phone.

"I thought, 'Holy crap, this really matters!'" Figliuolo told me later. "I had no idea people treasured these notes, and looked at them each day." What Mike and other effective managers realize is this: the most basic human need is validation. We all look forward to the praise we get from our team leaders. These regular acknowledgments are the key to keeping employees engaged. A sincere "thank you" reinforces good behavior and makes your staff even more committed to you and to the people they serve. This is a major building block of loyalty and trust.

Rule 2: Nurture Talent

Trainers know that they can change an animal's behavior through positive reinforcement, resulting in a happy, high-performing dog.

When you give the right feedback to your co-workers, you can often change the quality of their lives as well. When I was a senior director at First Brands, I hired a young engineer named Dave who was quiet but willing to stay with a project and work it from many different angles until it came to fruition. One day I asked him to come up with a way to reposition Jonny Cat, a cat litter product we had recently acquired from another company. At a time when all cat litter was pretty much viewed as nothing more than a bag of dirt, Dave tweaked the packaging and advertising so Jonny Cat would appeal to a higher-end market. He also helped to design a new facility to manufacture it. Soon after, I called him into my office. I told him that he had a rare gift for problem solving and I intended to put it to good use. This was a defining moment: Dave realized that his ideas could have an impact. Over the next few months, his confidence grew and he became a superb team leader. He soon took over my creativity seminars and later became an important member of DuPont's R&D team.

Praise, when given honestly and wholeheartedly, brings out the best in your staff, just as it brings out the best in any dog.

Rule 3: Go for Intrinsic Motivation

Agility trainers have something important to teach us about motivation. Consider how they get a dog to run an increasingly difficult course made up of hoops, planks, ladders, and tunnels at breakneck speed. First, they give the animal a treat each time it succeeds. Then, they reward the animals with a game of tug with a rope toy. Finally, they lead the dog through the different obstacles using only hand or body cues.

The treat and the toy are examples of extrinsic motivation. Later, the dogs make the leap to intrinsic motivation and begin performing for the sheer joy of it. They have discovered the thrill of the game and, from then on, they take pleasure in doing the job well.

In the business world, intrinsic motivation is the Holy Grail. It's widely believed to be the key to employee engagement, and one way to assure that people get the highest degree of satisfaction from their work.

Sociologists have long known that money isn't our sole motivation. We work because it brings us pleasure, because we get high on our own creativity or on helping others, or because we have a chance to make the world a better place.

Management gurus will tell you the same thing: we care just as much or more about meaning and a sense of mastery as we do about our paychecks. In fact, we perform better when we serve a higher goal, and we work even harder when we're offered an opportunity to learn and grow.

Medicine ranks highest of all professions in terms of intrinsic motivation; doctors and nurses are driven by the desire to heal and serve others. "Our people are highly altruistic and do the right thing for the right reasons," Zeev Neuwirth, chief of clinical effectiveness and innovation at Harvard Vanguard Health, the nation's first nonprofit HMO, said in an interview. "But they also want an opportunity to learn and to reach even higher levels of competence. That's why we set up our new Leadership Academy." During seventy-two hours of training over nine months, physicians in the program learn mentoring, negotiating, and coaching skills, as well as how to track the quality of health care and daily operations.

Fostering a high level of engagement and enthusiasm, Neuwirth believes, is the key to transforming the way we practice health care. "People outside of Harvard Vanguard come up to me and ask, 'What happened to those doctors? How can we accomplish the same thing at our organization?'" he said. "This program says, 'You can do it, we respect your ability. We want to work with you to make your practice the best in the country.'"

The same principles apply in the tech world. Netflix founder Reed Hastings believes the key to high performance is hiring the best and brightest and giving them free rein. Hastings started with an innovative marketing plan, then hired visionaries who wanted to change the way we package and deliver entertainment.

"The advantages of trusting people to manage their time are clear," Patty McCord, director of talent at Netflix, told *HR Magazine*. "We focus on what people get done, not how many hours or days they've worked. Have I ever fired a $100,000 employee for being tardy? No. Creative people come up with ideas outside of work."

How did Netflix come up with this organizational model? In the start-up phase, Hastings and McCord studied the kind of people they'd each successfully worked with in the past. They decided that what they valued was experience, so they set out to hire mature, accomplished, and self-directed people. Then they gave these people intellectual and operational carte blanche.

While other Silicon Valley companies offer free snacks and skateboards, "Netflix is more like a professional sports team," McCord said. "Satisfaction comes from the work, not the cookies."

"When we ask people why they chose us, they let us know that it's not for the money. It's for the other stuff," Allison Hopkins, vice president of human resources at Netflix, added. By that she means intrinsic motivation: the opportunity to work with absolute freedom with people at the very top of their game.

RULE 4: MAKE RELATIONSHIPS YOUR PRIMARY MOTIVATOR

And now we come to the principle so succinctly described by the novelist E. M. Forster: "Only connect."

Just as dogs blossom when they have a strong connection with their owners, employees blossom when they have a deep and meaningful connection with customers and coworkers.

There are some fascinating studies to support this. A team of researchers, led by Adam Grant at the University of Michigan, found that individuals who worked at call centers and ran mail-order businesses were happier and more productive if they had a chance to get to know the person on the other end of the phone. In a later study, Adam Grant and his colleagues at the Wharton School of the University of Pennsylvania arranged for college fund-raisers to talk with scholarship students about how they'd benefited from financial aid. The fund-raisers who spent a few minutes listening to these personal stories nearly tripled the pledges they brought in the following week.

In a wired economy, it's increasingly important to take the time to share our personal stories and find out what makes people tick.

Zappos founder Tony Hsieh understood this when he told his employees that their goal was to deliver happiness. Customers have used the Zappos web chat feature to share what they love about their watches, or why they admire their friend's taste in shoes. This isn't just a business; it's a social network.

And the ethos of being kind to one another online also spills over into ordinary life. In *Delivering Happiness*, Hsieh recounted the story of a worker who was standing in line at a grocery store when the elderly man in front of her came up short. She pitched in a few dollars, enabling him to complete his purchase, and told him not to pay her back, but to "pay it forward" and one day help somebody else. When the gentleman asked what prompted this act, she told him about the Zappos notion about delivering happiness. By chance, the Zappos employee ran into this man again, and he said he'd kept the tradition going. At Zappos, the staff doesn't just live for the paycheck. The best part of working there is the opportunity to be generous.

Rule 5: Reward the Pack

One of the biggest questions facing CEOs today is how best to reward and motivate employees when they can no longer afford to offer high-end perks.

Over the past five years, certain corporate benefits have declined. Contributions to an employee's 401(k) plan and reimbursement for taking continuing-education courses have been reduced, and there's no indication that these will be restored anytime soon. According to a 2009 survey reported in *The Wall Street Journal*, fringe benefits, from stock options to paid family leave and business-class travel, dropped significantly since 2005 and may plummet even lower.

"Benefits come back slowly when the labor market recovers," Peter Cappelli, George W. Taylor Professor of Management at the Wharton School of the University of Pennsylvania and director of the school's Center for Human Resources, told *The Wall*

Street Journal. While telecommuting has become a valued perk, employees are now more hesitant to be away from the office, fearing that when the next round of cuts are made those who put in more face time will be more favored.

All this can poke a big hole in your corporate culture.

According to a survey of *Fortune* magazine's "100 Best Companies to Work For," America's top CEOs have found creative ways to keep people happy and to show their gratitude. Here are some of their most ingenious solutions.

RULE 6: ELIMINATE THE DRUDGERY

One low-cost strategy, as we've seen, is to reward your staff by creating a more playful workplace. Another is by giving them a reprieve from their most hated tasks.

For example, the CEO of NetApp, a San Francisco data management company, has also released the staff from the drudgery of writing business plans, according to *Money* magazine. Instead, managers present "future histories" envisioning what their business will look like a year or two ahead. Other firms have streamlined paperwork and done away with interoffice memos.

Smart companies have also begun to let their crew off leash by giving people more time off for "good behavior." NetApp is one of many firms that gives workers time off to volunteer at their favorite charities.

"Firms that 'get it' are tapping into an individual's dreams and desires," Steve Arneson, PhD, president of Arneson Leadership Consulting, in Leesburg, Virginia, told me. "If one of your managers wants to go to the Super Bowl and you can find a way to make that happen, this is going to mean ten times more than a $2,500 bonus."

Rule 7: Keep Your People Healthy

Dogs protect us and, in return, we take responsibility for their health and well-being. Likewise, savvy companies care for their employees, offering everything from stress-reduction classes to on-site clinics. Wegmans Food Markets, for example, offers its employees a discount at its stores in addition to free yoga classes, according to *Money* magazine.

Pitney Bowes prides itself on having a "Culture of Health" and encourages employees to be screened for early signs of breast cancer and heart disease, according to Matt Broder, vice president of external communications. "An employee recently had a heart attack on premises," he recalled. "Our clinic got on the phone with the cardiologist and in less than an hour, our employee had a stent put in at the local hospital." This kind of personalized attention makes people feel not only appreciated, but well cared for.

Today's smart companies also cover big-ticket items for young families: staffers at NetApp, for example, are eligible to receive up to $11,390 to pay for adoption expenses per calendar year (with a $20,000 lifetime limit per family). They also get help treating autism, a benefit that has been used by more than forty employees to date, at a cost of nearly a quarter million dollars, according to *Money* magazine. The publication also notes that Boston Consulting Group offers first-class health coverage with a $5 copay, and also picks up 100 percent of any fertility treatments.

Companies that demand long hours and lots of travel have begun to say thank you with innovative programs like these, as well as with parental leave.

RULE 8: BLOW THEIR MINDS

There's a big difference between the mutt that sits home alone while his owner goes to work, and a dog that gets to roam and discover new sights and smells each day. The active dog will be more responsive as well as more motivated.

The corporate corollary is to encourage your staff to acquire new experiences. While tuition reimbursements have declined in recent years because they've grown too pricey, some firms send their top executives to TED (Technology, Entertainment, Design) conferences to learn about such engaging topics as rockets, bioengineering, robotics, and cosmology.

As *Businessweek* reported, a few years ago IBM took its top executives to the Vatican to view Michelangelo's frescoes and then held a series of workshops on innovation in Rome, the birthplace of the Renaissance. There, IBM managers met visionaries like Sunil Mittal, CEO of Bharti Airtel, an Indian tele-communications company that's adding more than a million customers a month; and Yang Mingsheng, president of the Agricultural Bank of China, who has started making microloans to peasant farmers. The creators of an in-house magazine called *Think*, IBM has long been clued into the greatest reward of all: the scent of new ideas.

If you can't bankroll a mind-blowing junket, there are other ways to teach your old dogs a few new tricks. Bring in outsiders for brown-bag lunches. Hold a series of seminars on problem solving and creativity. Take your team out of the office to brainstorm, or arrange an outing to the R&D department of a different industry. Build your corporate library and stock it with inspirational books. And set up a "corporate lattice" to give each staff member the opportunity to make a lateral move and spend time with a peer in another division or department.

Rule 9: Don't Forget Generation Y

Members of Generation Y seem to be the easiest to please, perhaps because they're just like puppies. They're young and enthusiastic, and everything seems fresh and new to them. "It takes very little to reward this generation," Donna Fenn reminded me. She cited the example of Undercurrent, a consulting company that pays special attention to this age group. Managers noticed that most of the younger staff members were leaving at about four o'clock each day. To encourage them to stay later, Fenn re-called, the managers bought a gigantic wall calendar covered with plastic bubble wrap. The last person to leave got to pop the bubble for that day of the week. Within a month, people were vying for this honor, and employees started lining up at the watercooler, asking, "How many bubbles did you pop this week?" It was a simple reward, she said. "It was fun. It was cheap, and it worked."

Team rewards appeal to members of Generation Y because they care about solidarity with the pack. In the old days, a manager singled out the top person with a bonus, which often made the other employ-ees resentful. Not so anymore. When smart manag-ers come to the end of a project, they might give the whole team a day off, send them to the movies, or hand out gift cards. "Gen Y responds to this. They also like small, frequent rewards," Fenn added.

Members of this generation are also easily en-gaged and love to be entertained. All you need to do is mix things up, too, so they don't get bored.

Chapter 8

Correct Early

B oth dogs and people have short memories for their mistakes. If you wait two weeks to tell your dog not to chew the furniture, he won't get the message. If you wait a few months to tell your employees they've messed up, they may feel angry or betrayed.

I learned the importance of this at the beginning of my career, when I was at Union Carbide. For nine months, I'd made ongoing presentations to upper management, laying out production lines with tape and arrows. One day, my boss called me in to talk about my performance and said, offhandedly, "Of course, you've been doing this all wrong." I was furious that he'd waited so long to explain the correct procedure. I was embarrassed by my failure to meet company standards and knew this evaluation might impact my raise and chances for promotion. Right then, I vowed to give staff members feedback as quickly as possible for whatever task they'd been assigned—not to micromanage them, but to guide them in a positive way.

Rule 1: Don't Save It for the Annual Review

I can't emphasize this enough: if you wait for the annual review to address things that your employees are doing wrong, it's hard to construct a coherent narrative. I've heard about managers who ricochet from praise to sullen disappointment in a single feedback session, leaving their direct reports disoriented and confused.

In a survey of human resources professionals by WorldatWork and Sibson Consulting, 58 percent graded their company's review procedures with a C or below. Many said they believe that the annual review does more harm than good   Only 30 percent of workers said they trusted the conventional review system. Others thought it was dishonest and lacked transparency. In fact, Samuel Culbert, a management professor at the University of California, Los Angeles, told *The New York Times* that it's time we did away with year-end reviews.

In *Get Rid of the Performance Review! How Companies Can Stop Intimidating, Start Managing—and Focus on What Really Matters*, Culbert explained that in the wrong hands, the annual performance review can become a tool for preening and for bullying. Today there's so much dread leading up to the annual review that HR directors are concerned that it contributes to the already rising level of employee stress.

So how can we make it easier—and less loaded— for managers to give feedback to their direct reports?

Once again we can take some tips from the most effective dog trainers:

- Speak up at the first sign of a problem.
- Focus on what the dog has the power to change.
- Identify specific steps that will lead to a better result.
- Make your dog feel that success is always within reach.
- Substitute the word "employee" in the above, and you have a guideline for good communication.

Receiving timely feedback is critical for employees to develop mastery over any complex task, according to Marguerite Moore Callaway, founder and president of the Callaway Leadership Institute, in San Rafael, California. "You have to know what you're doing well and when you've gone off track," she told me. "The trouble with performance reviews is that they're history lessons. They're about what didn't work in the past. They're also couched in anxiety, and that makes it tough for people to learn. You can't discover a new way of doing things in an atmosphere of fear."

As Callaway advised, "The key question you have to ask today is, Do your people understand how their work fits into a greater whole? Once they do, you get a high level of intrinsic motivation." And that makes the annual review a formality or even obsolete.

Rule 2: Avoid False Praise

When you're giving feedback, remember that you can destroy an employee just as easily with false praise or encouragement. If an employee repeatedly makes the same mistakes, you have nothing to gain by avoiding the situation. Smiling and acting patient can only make things worse.

When we got our first puppy, Samson, we loved everything about him. But the first time we left him home alone he chewed a hole in my wife's favorite comforter. When Brenda discovered this, she just cupped his face in her hands and told Samson that he shouldn't do this again. He licked her face and then went out to play.

The next time we left him in the house by himself, he chewed on our beautiful new wood coffee table. My wife again felt that a soothing chat with Samson was needed. Of course, that didn't work.

There were two problems with this approach. First was the timing—a puppy deals in the present. Second, a dog reacts more to *how* something is said than to what is said. You can shout "I love you" in a gruff voice, and your dog will shudder. At the same time, you can say, "You did wrong" in a pleasant voice, and he'll blithely go on making the same mistake.

Once we took this into account, Samson's behavior improved and we developed a more effective method of communication. (We'll always be grateful to our dogs for letting us practice with them before we had children.)

As a manager, you might try to don a mask of niceness and say soothing words, but the employee knows when underneath you're really seething.

"Praise first, criticize later" has long been the rule for employee feedback. We've just seen how praise can be misleading. Yet there are times when your kind words just don't penetrate.

For some time, HR folks have also touted "the criticism sandwich": start with a few kind words about the worker's performance, move on to their missteps, then wrap it up with praise. But according to Clifford Nass, a professor at Stanford University, most employees tune out the positive and hear only the reprimand.

Truth be told, managers probably invented "the criticism sandwich" to make themselves feel better. Why? Most people dislike conflict and confrontation and are hesitant to give bad news.

I tell my managers, "The best thing to do is treat your direct reports with respect but let them know when and how they're screwing up. That way they have the power to change the outcome." For communication to be effective, you have to keep it real.

Rule 3: Communicate with Gestures as Well as Words

We've spoken before about the importance of body language: often a simple gesture is enough to indicate that a worker has gone off track. A good trainer is in such close communication with his dogs that they can sense by the expression on his face when they're doing something wrong. Think of Special Agent Jethro Gibbs, played by Mark Harmon on the CBS television show *NCIS*. When Gibbs's mouth twitches, his team knows they're headed in the wrong direction and they instantly change course.

I have a similar "tell": when I'm not pleased with something, my eyebrows shoot up.

If you know your team well, their body language can give you a clue when things have gone off track. In a dog pack, a sudden flick of a tail, twitch of the ears, a ripple of fur are all signs of displeasure.

In meetings, I always watch my colleagues' faces for any indication of surprise or discomfort. I note where they stand in the room, whether they lean toward or away from the speaker, and whether their posture is relaxed. If my marketing director is pursing her lips and bowing her head, I know that she's not happy with the agenda and I need to ask her to weigh in. I also watch my board members for signs of fidgeting or boredom, and if I see any indication, I know it's time to cut my presentation short. The most important thing to note when you conduct a meeting is the flow of energy in the room. Cue into people's level of excitement. Make eye contact. Encourage participation. And when someone makes an important contribution, give her a positive sign—without interrupting her train of thought. When I hear a good suggestion, I become a true Italian and use my hands like I'm directing traffic near the Coliseum; my staff knows that I'm saying "Tell me more."

Chapter 9

Stay on Message

"Dogs like to know the rules," animal behavior expert Susan Tripp advises her clients. "They respond best when you give them a sense of purpose and a clear, consistent message."

Managers and CEOs must be consistent with their teams as well. The most successful business leaders articulate their corporate mission and communicate it at every level of the workplace. A number of companies, including FedEx, UPS, and Procter & Gamble, Genentech, W. L. Gore & Associates, the Container Store, and J. M. Smucker are all good role models. These firms, which have appeared on *Fortune* magazine's list of "100 Best Companies to Work For," have strong core values, and have spent a good deal of time defining their larger purpose.

RULE 1: TELL YOUR STORY

The happiest and most productive employees know both what's expected of them at work and also understand how their job fits into the larger purpose of the company.

Our mission at the American Pet Products Association remains constant. While providing the resources to make our members more successful, we also bring joy and companionship to people by providing for their pets. We work each day surrounded by our animals, and we sponsor ongoing studies on the special nature of the human-animal bond, exploring what dogs can teach us about healthy organizations and good leadership. That's what I call a consistent narrative.

W. L. Gore & Associates, makers of Gore-Tex, assembled an archive of 2,000 stories about "passionate champions" or highly engaged employees. Each of these stories served to underscore the corporate mission—to encourage teamwork and diversity and create a strong web of relationships.

Replacements, named one of the five most "psychologically healthy workplaces" in the United States in 2009 by the American Psychological Association, also considers itself culturally diverse. Although the company sells china, silverware, and glassware, it defines itself as being a place that "honors and preserves family traditions and connects their customers with their memories around the dinner table," human resources director Jeanine Falcon said. To achieve that, regular staff meetings are held in four languages—English, Spanish, Russian, and Serbo-Croatian—and courses in English as a Second Language are offered on-site. "We treat newcomers to our country with dignity and respect," Falcon added.

"After the Balkan conflicts in the 1990s, our town of Greensboro, North Carolina, had a huge wave of immigration," she explained. "We knew that if we landed in a new country tomorrow, we'd be pulling orders from a shelf, no matter how many degrees we had. So we made it a point to tell our new hires: 'We understand your situation. It doesn't matter where you come from. You deserve a good start.'"

When you communicate your core values, what you're really saying is: "We're about more than making money. We're a company with heart."

When Zappos founder Tony Hsieh asked his employees to do more with less, he also showed them he was willing to cut back as well. After the dot-com crash, he put his home and his savings on the line to build up inventory. When the company relocated from San Francisco to Las Vegas to further trim costs, seventy of its ninety employees came along. Moving wasn't a big deal, he wrote in *Delivering Happiness*, because the company was "like family." Employees described it as transplanting a tight-knit community "the size of a few square city blocks."

A report by Gallup on the state of the American workplace from 2008 through 2010 noted that "employees who feel supported and who feel valued are emotionally connected to their workplaces and have greater motivation to be productive."

What makes this possible? Being honest with your staff and keeping them informed. The Gallup poll found that employees who regularly hear the truth score higher on the optimism scale and tend to be more hopeful about the future, as well as more confident in their firm's ability to respond to challenges.

Aylwin B. Lewis, CEO of Sears Holdings, recently drew on his experience as a Baptist deacon to motivate a group of Kmart managers. "Our worst stores are dungeons!" he chanted, according to *Businessweek*. "Who wants to work in a dungeon? Who wants to work in an atmosphere that's going to suck the air out of the body?" A few minutes later, the managers—whom he'd just called on the carpet—were all hooting and hollering. Lewis got a standing ovation because he reminded his employees that their larger purpose was to create a welcoming environment. Since the merger of Kmart and Sears, Roebuck, Lewis's job has been to get all 330,000 employees excited and make them feel "like they're working for a start-up venture," even though the company routinely posts annual sales in the billions.

When you're a good communicator, you've mastered the art of making people happy, even when you're delivering bad news.

RULE 2: GET PERSONAL

Bill Gates got less-than-average grades for his communication skills as head of Microsoft; he could be boring, citing page after page of mind-numbing statistics, according to *Businessweek*. Or he could be curt, surly, and abrasive, as the world saw when his staff leaked a selection of sarcastic memos and they appeared on the website Gizmodo. But once Gates and his wife, Melinda, started the Gates Foundation, bringing medical care to third-world countries, this

CEO went to the head of his class and emerged as a great communicator. This is impressive when you consider that this guy was used to talking in terms of gigabytes and RAM and other trance-inducing technical details. But once he began talking about his passion, his whole demeanor changed: his face came alive and he was a more energetic public speaker. The first rule for engaging people is to begin with an idea you're committed to, and then let your audience know why you're doggedly pursuing it.

Rule 3: Keep It Simple

Jack Welch, former CEO of GE, made it to the top because he insisted on straightforward communication. He would have made a great dog trainer because he was big on consistency and told everyone to "keep it simple." One of his most memorable quotes: "Insecure managers create complexity." Welch felt that the plainer the message, the easier it was for people to live up to high expectations.

Steve Jobs is aptly called a Silicon Valley evangelist because he's consistently telling people how his latest technology is going to change the world. Jobs knows that "staying on message" is what helps you sell effectively.

Rule 4: See the Bigger Picture

When an industry is in crisis, a good communicator reaches out to the public and opens up a dialogue.

For weeks, BP's Tony Hayward, who hemmed and hawed and generally looked helpless, was the most hated CEO in America for his company's role in the Gulf oil spill in 2010.

Contrast that to the proactive approach taken by Shell's former CEO John Hofmeister, who in 2005 embarked upon a fifty-city tour across the country to discuss America's energy crisis, answering questions from the audience. After retiring in 2008, he started a foundation called Citizens for Affordable Energy, to consider the role not just of oil, but of coal, geothermal energy, and biofuels in our national energy policy. While Hayward seemed to shrink in the public eye, Hofmeister stepped forward and took control of the conversation. What's more, he was honest about what Big Oil could and couldn't do—noting that it was only one part of the energy solution.

RULE 5: DEFINE THE MISSION

How do you come up with a mission or a set of core values that engages all your employees? Here's a good example. A few years ago, workers at Molson Coors began the bloodhound process of "clue gathering," i.e., finding facts about the company that contributed to its overall culture. The company then initiated a program called "Pub Talk," encouraging leaders to convey objectives in plain language and replace business jargon like "core competencies" with the phrase "what we do well." As a result, memos were no longer filled with arcane technical terms, and people began to hash out their issues face-to-face at "Pub Talk" meetings.

What's the secret to these communication programs? Here's what we learn from man's best friend:

- Be an empathetic listener (just note how a dog cocks his head toward you when you talk).
- Go beyond your words and tone—consider how your intentions might be perceived.
- Stay engaged—like a dog, you should always look for clues and share feedback with others.

Rule 6: Involve Everybody—Right Down to the Warehouse Worker and the Security Guard

Sunshine Makers, which produces cleaning products under the Simple Green brand, has built its corporate culture from the ground up and involves its workers in every level of the business. Denise Dochnahl, the company's marketing specialist, notes, "Bruce FaBrizio, our CEO, manages by wandering around and listening to people. And by that, I mean everyone."

When FaBrizio announced a company-wide contest to come up with a theme for a new TV and print campaign, "only a few folks responded," Dochnahl recalls. "Some begged off, thinking, 'Advertising isn't my area of expertise.'" So our CEO called the staff together and said, "'This contest is for everybody, I want you to help us craft our message. That means feedback from the warehouse, the mail room, the security guards, our marketing team, and the customer service reps. And remember, people, the cash reward is pretty big.'"

"When new employees come on board," Dochnal added, "we make sure they understand how much we value their input. We also have an online program called Success Factors where workers set goals and review their progress with their managers."

This kind of clear, consistent communication increases employee motivation and participation, and contributes to a strong corporate culture.

Each year, I host a series of meetings with my staff to come up with our narrative for the year. We consider how we're going to adjust our goals to keep up with the changing economy. Then we identify two to three key goals.

When I first joined the American Pet Products Association, it served only American companies. Yet in one of these "vision meetings," my staff convinced me we should start accepting members from Europe and China. I took their recommendations to the board, and they became excited about global outreach. We could boost membership by at least 25 percent, which would translate into more sales and services for our members. Since we went international, APPA members have had a steady increase in orders—in fact, we're one of the few industries that appears to be recession-resistant. And since then, my staff has played an essential role in strategic planning.

They know that they can help shape the big picture, and then be responsible for making it happen.

When things go wrong, it's often because a CEO or manager has changed direction and failed to bring his people along. The result is a communications vacuum. That, as Jack Welch warned, gives rise to chaos.

As animal behavior expert Susan Tripp has said: "Dogs are always trying to figure out the rules of the road. If you don't give them the structure they need to be comfortable, they'll create their own."

People are no different. To perform to the best of their ability, employees need a clear, consistent mandate. They need to know not only what their duties are, but how they fit into the larger purpose of the organization.

RULE 7: SOLICIT FEEDBACK

The best way to keep everyone on the same page is to regularly ask your employees the following questions:

- Do you know what's expected from you on this project?
- Do you have the resources you need to do your job?
- Are you passionate about your work?
- Are you getting the feedback and recognition you need to stay engaged?
- Do you have a strong personal rapport with colleagues?

- Do you have a best friend at the office?
- Does your manager support your growth and development?
- Have you learned something new in the past year?
- Do you feel that your ideas and suggestions count?
- Do you know how your work supports the larger mission of the company?

A growing number of companies now solicit this kind of feedback once a year. If your employees can answer all these questions positively, that's an indication that you're a strong communicator and that you're giving your pack all the cues they need to rank among the "Best in Show."

Chapter 10

Lead by Example

A nyone who has raised more than one dog at a time knows that the older one will always teach the younger one the household rules. This makes the younger dog feel secure, and contributes to a stable and harmonious environment.

Similarly, each new employee needs a mentor who can answer practical questions and also introduce them to the corporate culture.

Recent studies show that standard orientation programs are barely adequate. "The most frequent complaints about new employee orientation are that it is overwhelming, boring, or that the new employee is left to sink or swim," according to Judith Brown, senior compliance specialist for human resources, national security programs at AECOM, a technological and management support service firm. "The result is often a confused new employee who is not productive and is more likely to leave the organization within a year."

Smart companies have strong orientation programs that quickly get new hires up to speed.

What happens when new workers are left completely on their own? Let me tell you a story.

A friend recently adopted a shelter dog, named Jake, who wasn't used to being left alone. Jake startled easily. He barked whenever the phone rang or whenever someone came to the front door. It turned out that he'd been raised with an older dog that had acted as his protector. When the other dog was around, Jake looked to him for cues and then learned how to respond. Without that feedback, however, Jake was lost.

My friend now had the daunting task of learning how to "speak dog," and give Jake the same kind of reassurance he got from the older dog. Alone in the house with her, Jake tended to be anxious. But as soon as she took him to the dog park, he relaxed. He befriended a rottweiler with a strong personality. From then on, he had a dog he could look up to and his skittishness abated. In the company of other canines, he seemed happy and well adjusted. In short, he was fine as long as he had a mentor. Good managers play the same role for the employees. Their primary role is to interpret signals from colleagues and from outside competitors and tell the pack how to respond. People also look to them for guidance when deciding how to deal with unexpected challenges.

Three years ago, I had a crisis on my hands. An investment banker wanted to bring his children to the Global Pet Expo, our annual industry trade show. As I entered the registration area, I heard this man yelling at my staff, "Kids are future pet owners! How can you ignore them? They're potential customers!" I gently inserted myself into the conversation and explained that this was the one time our members could show their wares to potential buyers and that we couldn't allow children on the exhibition floor for both safety and insurance reasons.

My staff was clearly hoping this would defuse the situation, but then the guy started jumping up and down like Rumpelstiltskin. "I'm going to tell my colleagues to boycott your Expo," he said. "In fact, I'm going to start my own trade show! We'll see how long you stay in business!"

At this point, I smiled at him and said, "You know, I've got a really great staff here. They're the best in the business. If you decide to start your own Expo, we'd be happy to help you out!"

For a moment he was speechless. So I quickly added, "You know, we'd be glad to watch your kids while you attend the trade show. We have a play room set up for that. And this year's Expo is amazing. You won't want to miss it." Once we'd offered to entertain his children, the broker relented. He spent the whole day at the Expo, looking at everything from doggie underwear to lizard jewelry. Six months later, he invested in three companies whose products he'd seen at the trade show.

In the meantime, my staff realized that you don't have to let a situation escalate, nor do you have to accept a tirade of abuse.

This was an example of what I call the "big dog" response. How many times have you seen a German shepherd or a Lab just stand there, while a terrier dances around him and keeps yapping? The big dog knows he doesn't have to do a thing. So he doesn't react at all. He just projects a calm, assertive energy and waits for things to return to normal.

The Great Chain of Mentoring

The ability to be calm in a moment of crisis is a skill I learned from an "old dog"— a manager who'd seen everything and who was a terrific mentor.

When I joined the marketing department at First Brands, I worked for a guy named Dick Watt. The company was full of "helicopter bosses" who hovered over your shoulder every minute and tried to meddle with your work. But Watt was different. He gave us a long leash and encouraged us to take risks, even if that meant pursuing some outlandish ideas for a new marketing campaign. If we messed up, he never lost his temper. He'd just sit there calmly and say, "Okay, what can we learn from this?"

Our group was under extraordinary pressure; if product sales went down, we got the blame. But Watt exuded confidence. He always stood up for us and gave us honest feedback, but he never pulled his punches. And he didn't consider himself above the rules; he worked sixteen-hour days like the rest of us. And he helped us deal with the other managers we reported to.

One day he faced down a snarling vice president, and insisted he let us complete our marketing campaign. Some of the top people doubted us and thought our whole approach was crazy. But this particular product launch turned out to be a resounding success.

With Dick in mind, I sat down and made a list of all the qualities employees want to see in their leaders. I came up with the following:

- Calm, assertive energy
- Loyalty to the pack
- A good sense of humor
- Stamina, perseverance, and the willingness to work as hard as everyone else
- Straightforwardness and honesty
- Intuition and the ability to read others' intentions
- Consistency in giving feedback
- Decisiveness
- Openness to change
- Good impulse control and a high tolerance for stress

These traits form the acronym CLASSIC DOG and are the basis of effective leadership.

Who Needs Mentoring?

Bosses used to have more time to mentor their employees. "If you go back a generation ago, your immediate supervisor had the responsibility to develop you," Peter Cappelli, a professor of management at the Wharton School of the University of Pennsylvania, wrote in his blog. In those days, bosses "knew how to give employees a chance to accomplish things."

Many companies rely on informal mentoring programs and leave these teaching relationships to chance. But mentorship from an "older dog" has become increasingly important as younger employees enter a tight job market. We thought members of Generation Y would be on the move every two years, jumping from one job to the next. But the old rule of thumb—seven to nine jobs by the time you're thirty-five—is no longer valid. Today's young people hope to get lucky and stay with a single firm for several years. Promotions aren't something they can take for granted. Variety will come, not from moving up the corporate ladder, but moving to another place on the corporate lattice and taking a job elsewhere in the company. That means they'll need someone to show them the ropes.

What about employees who are feeling over-worked and underappreciated? Four in ten workers today complain that their companies are understaffed, according to a recent Gallup poll, and on-the-job stress is their biggest worry. A formal mentoring program goes a long way toward making these folks feel valued and appreciated.

But there's a rub. Peter Cappelli noted that while dealing with outsourcing and downsizing, bosses have forgotten how to be good mentors. "If you go back a generation ago, your immediate supervisor had the responsibility to develop you," he wrote. Bosses "knew how to give employees a chance to accomplish things." Slowly the tradition of mentorship eroded and became more "low-impact." Instead of a trusted guide, you turned to your peers to bounce off your new ideas, or went to multiple people for advice.

In fact, developing a formal mentoring system at your company should be a priority because such a program can improve the success rates for mentors as well as for those being mentored. A five-year study at Sun Microsystems showed that workers who participated in a mentorship program had five times more pay raises than the control group. The mentors themselves had almost six times the pay raises of peers who didn't participate in the program. No wonder 71 percent of all Fortune 500 companies now encourage such relationships.

Intel is taking a fresh approach to this age-old practice. At the company's chip-making facility in New Mexico, newcomers are matched with "people mentors" who can plug them into a web of diverse corporate relationships, providing connections through social networking on Circuit, Intel's employee website. Instead of being matched with another employee who has similar duties and responsibilities, new employees can go online to find a potential mentor and click on topics they want to discuss, like leadership or culture.

By design, Intel's program connects employees around the world. Moreover, according to an article in *Fast Company* magazine, the company uses written contracts and tight deadlines to make sure this mentoring program gets results and spreads "best practices" throughout the organization. Intel is also beginning to experiment with group mentoring, with one manager initiating several new recruits.

Harris Bank takes a similar approach. When a bell rings to signal the beginning of a round of "speed mentoring," top executives from different departments, one per table, field questions from as many as seven employees. After ten minutes, the pack moves on to "interview" a manager from another department.

Similar to speed dating, this process energizes employees and is the fastest way to expose new employees to the many different kinds of expertise required to run a $43 billion company.

The bank also encourages peer-to-peer mentoring. When Judith Rice left her job as the top aide to Chicago mayor Richard Daley, she asked one of her new coworkers at the bank to be her "executive coach" and help her transition to working in the private sector from the public sector. Today, Rice mentors other women in the firm, and also reaches out to women who run community groups, offering guidance and support.

This program "makes mentoring accessible to our entire employee population," Deirdre Drake, the bank's senior vice president of human resources services, told *U.S. Banker*. It also makes employees "think harder about their potential and their possibilities."

In addition, mentoring programs can reduce turnover and help you retain your best hires. Deloitte & Touche, a global accounting and management consulting firm, has set up an online coaching program so virtual mentors can help employees define their goals and figure out how to do their best work. This program, open to everyone at the company, saves more than a thousand jobs per year, according to W. Stanton Smith, who was a principal in human resources at Deloitte & Touche.

When I talk about great mentoring, Murray Martin, chairman, president, and CEO of Pitney Bowes, Inc., comes to mind. Martin learned everything he needed to know about business from his father, who helped him launch a dog-breeding venture. Martin got his first crack at being CEO at the age of five.

"I wanted a puppy and my father said, 'Well, you can have one, but you've got to pay for it,'" Martin told *Forbes* magazine. "My father taught me basic business practices. Nothing was free. He charged me rent for the barn and if I used a piece of wood or some wire, I had to pay for it—and for dog food. It took me almost two years before I got my first financial reward, when the first litter of pups sold to repay my debt. Then I turned profitable. I understood financing and how you pay for things. Eventually we were raising forty to fifty dogs a year and selling them all over Canada."

While raising dogs, Martin learned how to do bookkeeping as well as how to manage money, advertise his product, and distribute it. "I was lucky to have a father who understood those things and was willing to spend time to teach me," he said. "It was fun, and it let me acquire capabilities that others didn't have at such a young age...including the importance of understanding your customers."

His advice to employees echoes those lessons he learned from raising dogs: "Know your territory.

Carve out a space that you understand. Then see how you can apply that knowledge in other areas."

Getting New Dogs Up to Speed

If you want a dog to walk by your side, instead of pulling you along like the tail end of caboose, you need to spend about eight weeks on obedience training. If you want to teach a search-and-rescue dog how to enter crumbling buildings, you'll need to invest at least twenty-five weeks.

When I was a vice president in charge of human resources, I discovered that the same kind of learning curve applies to employees. It takes anywhere from eight to ten weeks to get an entry-level clerk up to speed, and nearly twenty-six weeks to fully orient a product designer or high-level engineer, according to a 2003 study by Mellon Financial Corp.

People often ask how to get the best from new hires. Here are a few guidelines to consider, regardless of your training program's duration.

1. Don't overload new hires with information. Studies show that handing out too many thick reports and orientation materials can make people feel overwhelmed.

2. Plug them into a social network. Give them a chance to sniff around and find out who does what in the company. Once they have a good map of the ter-

ritory, they'll know where to take their questions.

3. Encourage peer and group mentoring on the company intranet, or create chat rooms where employees can explore different departments or seek advice.

4. Give newcomers assignments that will help them build relationships. The standard operating procedures tend to be small, compact, and easily achieved. But researchers at Babson College have found that people get on board faster when they're asked to tackle more ambitious projects that require them to reach deep into an organization to find answers.

5. In addition to a mentoring program, consider a buddy system, where newcomers can quickly get answers to common questions like, "How do I order office supplies?" and "Who really has the power to make decisions here?"

6. Tell your newcomers not to go for brownie points. Choosing a mentor for political reasons is a bad idea. Workers, at any level, need someone they can trust and ask for help, not someone they can manipulate.

Companies are increasingly turning to virtual mentoring and even matching people up online to avoid turning mentoring into a popularity contest. The idea isn't to create a dynasty, but to build a tight-knit and collaborative team that functions like a pack of dogs, even if the team reaches across the usual departmental lines.

Encourage Intelligent Disobedience

What about times when you want your employees to be confident enough to break the rules? Intelligent disobedience, a concept from the dog world, applies to the business world as well.

Guide dogs for the blind have to protect their charges from danger, like a car jumping a curb or running a red light. Trainers know it's impossible to prepare these dogs for every challenge, so they teach the animals to follow their instincts and make creative choices, even if that means ignoring owners' commands.

In enlightened companies, the person with the courage to disobey can turn out to be a hero as well—employees with the courage to ignore your instructions can save you from making a big mistake.

One day, I gave Sal, my most gifted engineer at First Brands, the blueprint for a production line. He looked over it and said, "No way is this going to work." I told him not to worry.

Instead, he ignored my directive and made some crucial corrections to my design. On the first day of operation, he walked me through the line and showed me where I'd inadvertently created a physically impossible task. According to the blueprint, the motions required to get the plastic bags coming off the line into the box would likely result in a packer dislocating his shoulder. By fixing the problem without asking my permission, Sal had saved me from a costly error.

The smart manager rewards that kind of behavior. If you value intelligent disobedience, then people will have the confidence to act decisively *before* things go wrong.

Intelligent disobedience isn't about being contrary or difficult; it's about doing what's best for the company, even if it goes against the boss's orders. Here are some examples of when it works.

1. When an employee breaks a rule to help a customer

Most retailers allow returns within a set period of time, accompanied by a store receipt. But savvy retailers allow clerks to use their own judgment. When my wife, Brenda, took a pair of running shoes back to the New Balance store, she didn't have her receipt and was probably past the store's "return by" date. The employee allowed her to return the shoes anyway, and the company gained our loyalty for life.

A good customer service rep will acknowledge the problem and then do something above and beyond the call of duty. When that happens, your grateful customer—if you're lucky—might share the positive experience with friends on Facebook or Twitter. These days the buzz you get on social media is even better than ad time for the Super Bowl.

2. When there's an opportunity you can't refuse

Each year the American Pet Products Association runs a poetry contest about pets that's open to students in the third, fourth, and fifth grades. During the contest's second year, we were looking for new ways to promote it. While I was out of town, Jenn, our public relations manager, saw an opportunity that was too good to resist. She went over budget, spending $3,000 on a booth at an event sponsored by the American Kennel Club to reach 35,000 dog owners, many of whom would bring their children to the show. This is a fine example of intelligent disobedience. The smart CEO builds in a margin for this kind of cost overrun.

3. When you're in a crisis

The pet food contamination scare in 2007 was one of the toughest challenges our industry has dealt with in recent years. We have rules for who can respond to media inquiries. In this case, the Pet Food Institute (PFI) was first on the list since it represents the largest manufacturers. However, when the news broke, I'd just given several media interviews about other topics. Suddenly, ABC, NBC, and *The Today*

Show were asking me to comment on the news since they hadn't been able to reach anyone else in the industry for a statement. I went on the record, saying, "We will recall any product we even suspect might be affected. Our first allegiance is to you and to your pets. And we will make sure that this never happens again."

This was a tense moment. I'd taken a position that was outside my authority and was worried about the APPA board's reaction. But with this initial response to satisfy the immediate demands of the press, PFI and others had more time to gather facts and give a complete response. The public's reaction was positive, and the industry was helped because someone had quickly responded compassionately to pet owners.

4. When you're problem solving

Intelligent disobedience is also at the root of creativity. You have to reject the rules if you want to build something new. To improve a product or a methodology, you have to throw away the original template and let go of your assumptions. That's how my team at First Brands came up with the zipper-locking bag. And we had other successes, using the same approach.

Another of our products, Prestone Antifreeze, came in a bright yellow jug, which customers complained about, saying the liquid often splattered when the customer tried to funnel it into the car radiator. Our CEO asked R&D to design a new container, but nothing they came up with worked. I soon found myself in a room with a group of engineers, and we were told, "Fix the problem."

First, we threw out all the conventional approaches, then, over the next few hours, came up with Prestone in a plastic bag, Prestone in a box, and even Prestone in a sock. Finally, we asked ourselves what these solutions had in common. The answer was better airflow! We could keep the yellow jug if we changed the shape of the handle. It worked! By ignoring the rules, we kept our iconic packaging and kept the brand intact.

How to Teach Intelligent Disobedience

Independent thinking is a prerequisite for innovation, but "today's leaders get little training in this," according to Steve Arneson, a management consultant and author of *Bootstrap Leadership: 50 Ways to Break Out, Take Charge, and Move Up*. "In the corporate world, we do a terrible job of teaching it. But companies are now beginning to ask, 'How can we create an environment that supports innovation and creativity?'"

Pepsi, Google, and Apple are among the companies that do this well, Arneson noted. They aren't afraid of pushback. "The connection is clear," he said. "Find the innovative company and you've found a place that fosters intelligent disobedience. That's the key to producing multiple ideas."

A.G. Lafley, former CEO of Procter & Gamble, had the courage to go against the industry norms. After taking the helm in 2000, he reated a hotline for inventors and consumers. With this, Procter & Gamble became one of the first companies to solicit new product ideas not just from its own R&D unit, but from the general public. The innovation team now reviews ideas that come from any country in the world.

To be a leader in innovation, you have to be a bloodhound—constantly following your nose, moving into unsafe or uncharted territory, and taking some calculated risks. Good CEOs like Larry Ellison of Oracle and Steve Jobs of Apple have rebellious streaks and are constantly reinventing their products and redefining the marketplace. That may be easy to do in an evolving field like technology. But Wal-Mart, the world's largest retailer, keeps reinventing itself as well: in 2010, the company announced a global commitment to sustainable agriculture, including an emphasis on purchasing more items from small and midsized farmers around the world and reducing food waste.

Recently, savvy business leaders have begun to adopt the phrase "intelligent disobedience" as an alternative to the shopworn phrase "think outside the box" because it conveys the gutsiness required to break the rules—even the prime directive that says "profits first."

Value Independent Thinking

Managers can teach intelligent disobedience the same way a dog handler does. You need to indicate that this is acceptable behavior, and identify the circumstances in which independent thinking is both valued and required.

Leadership expert Bruna Martinuzzi, writing in her blog, offered some guidelines for encouraging intelligent disobedience, and to her list I've added a few of my own:

1. Consider decentralizing your decision making and encourage those closest to the problem to come up with solutions on the spot.

2. Be open to new challenges and new ideas, no matter where they come from.

3. Help your staff to understand the difference between facts and assumptions. Encourage them to test their ideas to see what really works.

4. Beware of rules, regulations, and habits that lead to blind conformity. The worst reason to do something is often because "everybody else is doing it." That holds true for the day-to-day operation of your company, as well as for the way you position yourself within the marketplace.

5. Remember the lesson of the seeing-eye dog and don't be afraid to surround yourself with people who are smarter than you are: intelligent disobedience is what can save you from your own blind spots.

6. Put outcomes before compliance. Look at the results, not at whether your policy manual was followed to a "T."

7. Reward people who have the courage to take risks if their actions serve the greater good.

8. Watch how often you say no. Make sure you aren't closing off new avenues of exploration. If you have to reject an idea, give your people some wiggle room to explore and check out new alternatives.

9. Remember that your job isn't just to secure the bottom line; it's to protect the welfare of the pack. When someone balks at your orders, it may be because you haven't considered the effect of a new policy or procedure on the people who actually have to carry it out.

10. Give a prize each month to the person who bent the rules and got the best result!

The Difference Between Good and Great

ESI International, a global management solutions company based in Arlington, Virginia, reported that good project managers—who have to deliver goods on time, keep an eye on costs, and look out for the well-being of their staff—often practice intelligent disobedience by doing the following:

- Stating unpopular options
- Standing up to senior management
- Bending the rules, as necessary, to get the job done
- Coming up with compelling arguments to get additional backing and support

If you're in charge of a project or division, I guarantee that there will be times when you'll need to have the courage and the confidence to stand up for your team, fend off obstacles to your success, and argue for new approaches that, while untested, are likely to promote your company's mission and objectives. People who practice intelligent disobedience need to be exceptional communicators who can make their purpose clear.

They're also the kind of executives who tend to get ahead. An intelligently disobedient leader comes up with a plan of action, looks for obstacles, and finds a way to work around them. Leaders like this are far more likely to ask, "How can we do it?" than to say, "Here a five good reasons we shouldn't move ahead." They're also likely to surround themselves with people who share their passion and their commitment to "do what it takes" to get the job done.

Know Your Coworkers

Debra Tosch, executive director of the Search Dog Foundation, has, along with her trained search-and-rescue dog, helped firefighters at Ground Zero and aided workers during Hurricane Katrina and volunteers who flocked to Haiti after the island's devastating earthquake in 2010.

"I have a bond with my dog, and a level of trust that's extraordinary," Tosch said. "Once we've trained rescue dogs, these animals make their way through piles of rubble where human beings can't go," she explained. "We can call them back, but we also have to trust them to make the decision whether to abandon their post. They'll stay in a search area if they think they've located a survivor. The only reason I can sleep at night, when I'm on this kind of job, is that I know my dog will do whatever it takes to find somebody who's still down there, even it means ignoring my commands."

Managers need to have the same unshakeable trust in their key people. To foster intelligent disobedience, you have to know when to cut your people loose from ordinary rules and regulations. In the long run, it's all about having a solid partnership.

The questions I ask you now are these: Do you have as much faith in your employees as Debra has in her dog? Do you trust your people to do the right thing in a crisis? Are you overly concerned with getting them to do things right? Or are you also training them to disobey when it serves the common good?

Chapter 12

Bad Dog, Bad Hire

S o far, we've been talking about the finest qualities of man's best friend. Now it's time to take a look at the more troublesome habits we see in our canine companions.

"Bad dog" behavior can wreak havoc in any household. And it can severely hamper any organization as well.

Here's a list of "bad dog" qualities to look for and to avoid, when interviewing job candidates:

- Poor temperament—acting surly with others
- Superdominant behavior
- Needy or spoiled behavior
- Destructive tendencies

Now let's discuss each one in detail and see how they can be eliminated.

Poor Temperament

My friend Jack worked in the marketing department of a large consumer products company. His boss liked to say no. If a project wasn't his idea or he couldn't find a way to take credit for it, he'd find a way to sink it. Often he'd end up sitting on everyone's best work. "He put my reports aside or let them languish in a drawer," Jack said. "And when I protested, he called me the world's biggest pain in the ass."

After a few months of this, Jack left that department and went back to his old job in R&D. A few weeks later, two other colleagues left as well.

By nature, Jack's boss was difficult and withholding, and liked to take his frustration out on others. For years, employees had been complaining about this manager, but nothing happened. Finally, he was stripped of his responsibilities as a supervisor and moved into a job where he worked alone. By then, his toxic behavior had cost the company hundreds of thousands of dollars—he'd lowered his department's productivity and created a pattern of high turnover. I always wondered why it took the firm so long to put this person in a cage where he could no longer snap at others.

Junior staff can be just as troublesome and difficult. I once hired a charming administrator who delighted in turning people against each other, but it took us all a while to catch on to her true nature. The tipping point was when she was asked to notify exhibitors of a last-minute change in the registration process before our trade show. When she fouled up, she blamed someone else who wasn't even in her department—a young trainee whom I knew and trusted. Then the administrator hid in the hallway and, with a big smile on her face, watched as the unsuspecting employee got called on the carpet. There was no way around it: this administrator was a liar and an instigator, and it was time to throw her out.

These two case histories both required swift action. You can't afford to dally when you're dealing not only with bad habits, but with serious character flaws as well.

Superdominant Behavior

I once collaborated on a project with a CEO who had to be the alpha dog at every meeting. He took over a firm that had been on the verge of bankruptcy for five years and wanted to be viewed as its savior. If anyone tried to make a constructive suggestion, he'd muscle them out of the way. During planning meetings, he'd strut around like a show dog and make promises he'd fail to keep. All we could do was bide our time and try to work around him until the board stepped in and found a suitable replacement. In the meantime, he made my job much harder. This CEO had deceived a lot of people into thinking that he was competent, but underneath the "top dog" posturing and dominance was a small dog that felt terrified and insecure.

Some advice to boards: look out for the candidate who starts every sentence with the word "I," makes golden promises, and has no backup plan. Once these people get entrenched in an organization, it's hard to get them out. The only recourse is to wait for them to fail at something big, so you have "just cause."

Needy or Spoiled Behavior

At least one-third of the people in the workforce these days would line up to tell their bosses, "You never listen to my ideas," "I need more support on this project," or "You don't pay me enough." These employees need a lot of hand-holding, no matter what you do or how much you give them.

One solution is to institute a buddy system. Pair them up with a mentor, or even a peer, and ask them to check in with you once a week, and make note of their progress. This is an easy way to ensure that those who need a more regular pat on the back are getting what they need.

In the past I've made an effort to soothe those who complain constantly. I once shared an administrative assistant with another vice president. I was careful to thank her and to praise her work, and she still came up with the same old litany: "You give me too much to do. I can't be expected to type your letters *and* answer the phone." Eventually, the vice president and I realized she was giving us both the same speech to use against each other.

People who feel overworked and overburdened are always with us; their complaints might seem louder today because, for many, their workload *has* increased. They just don't realize that we're all in the same boat, so it's important for managers to be strong mentors who help these individuals understand what's expected of them and of the staff as a whole. Employees need to feel a part of a group effort, just as they need to be aware that being vocal about their discomfort affects everyone at the company. The best indication of whether any of these people can be saved is whether they're willing to change.

Destructive Tendencies

Consider the dog that seems well behaved but chews the rug or pulls down the drapes the moment he's left alone. A destructive animal goes on a rampage with no warning, leaving havoc in his wake. Unfortunately, there are people like this, too.

The workers who never tell you there's a problem can turn out to be dangerous. I remember a maintenance mechanic at Union Carbide who secretly nursed a grudge against the company. He failed to adjust the production line to avoid a potential accident, and later refused to clean up a leak that he could have easily prevented. This kind of employee is a much bigger problem than the complainer, who at least tells you about the perceived problems. An employee with destructive tendencies will instead appear to be doing his job, perhaps even smiling occasionally, when in fact he's spending his time thinking of ways to undermine you. My advice: don't give folks like this a second chance. If you do, they're likely to find a way to hurt you or a member of your crew.

When this mechanic later failed to replace a broken screw, the line went down, and our most important piece of machinery was permanently damaged. Although his actions had cost the company thousands of dollars, I didn't immediately fire him. I had to investigate the incident first. When I realized that he'd let something slide on purpose, I let him go.

"Bad dog" behavior can throw your organization into disarray. A good human resources department can help you to avoid these situations. And if you're smart, you'll put a lot of time and money into selecting your employees. Yet even with the sophisticated testing we have today, hiring remains an art.

When we fail to find a good fit, there's a big price to pay. In my experience, it costs about $17,000 to replace the average worker, but the costs get higher as you go up the ladder. You have to figure on spending $38,000 to replace an executive making $60,000 per year, while replacing an executive vice president can run much more. That's the main reason we take so long to give someone the boot.

However, I've also seen managers give up too quickly, when only a few adjustments may be needed to get a worker up to speed. So when should you nurture someone and give them a second chance? And when do you give up?

My advice: watch how other employees respond to the worker in question. When your employees approach you with vague complaints about someone, seem anxious when around this individual, or try to avoid the colleague, it's time to act.

The important thing is to differentiate between "bad dogs" that are likely to destroy or somehow harm the pack and those that need more training and attention.

When I took over the Oil-Dri legal department, I inherited an assistant I'll call "Cathy." She was so blunt that people didn't want to work with her. Because she had no people skills, my first impulse was to let her go; yet as I watched her work, I realized that she knew how to organize the cases, gather data, and resolve frivolous complaints. She was good at her job and I didn't want to lose her. So I asked if she'd be willing to take a class in human relations. Cathy agreed, and while she didn't suddenly transform into the most likeable person on the planet, she gained enough tact that my staff accepted her and no longer saw her as the enemy.

What else can you do to help salvage a bad hire? Find someone in your organization to serve as an unofficial role model for the difficult employee. Pair them together on a short-term project. If the bad hire has enough good qualities, he'll respond to being mentored.

I've heard that Warren Buffett once boasted that he never had to fire anybody. He just moved his people around within the company and found them better jobs. Often it's a case of matching the personality to the task and also learning whether people play well with others or work best alone.

Deposing a Bad CEO

We've talked about how to handle bad behavior in the rank and file, but what about dealing with a difficult, distracted, or incompetent CEO? Once again, dogs have something to teach us. They won't follow an unstable leader. Only humans will.

Because we rely too much on our reasoning skills, rather than our instincts, we tend to make excuses for a greedy, abusive, or incompetent boss. How else do we explain the unchecked reign of CEOs like James Cayne, who according to Reuters, played in a poker tournament while his investment bank, Bear Stearns, went down the tubes? Or Dennis Kozlowski, CEO of Tyco, who furnished his Mediterranean-style villa with a $15 million interest-free loan and threw himself a $2 million birthday party, all from company funds?

Bad CEOs like to rule through intimidation, so removing these top dogs can be tricky. Executives who report directly to them are often afraid of losing their jobs by sounding the alarm, or might be so beaten down that they no longer have the will or courage to resist. Some CEOs threaten to retaliate and make life miserable for those who challenge them. Others prefer to remain in the dark. It's as if they're saying: "Don't you dare give me bad news!"

Bad CEOs deceive and abuse their employees until they break their spirits. Boards need to be alert for leaders who criticize or intimidate their staff in public must be told, "This is not the way we do things." A good board will stop renegade or predatory leaders before they have a chance to run their people—and the firm—into the ground.

One of the most valuable things I've learned over the years is that you can't expect underlings to dislodge or overthrow an incompetent leader. Chief executives have to be replaced by their own pack, not subordinates.

A while back, there was a lot of grumbling about Jonathan Schwartz at Sun Microsystems. Employees complained anonymously on Glassdoor, a free website where people can post reviews of their employers, about Schwartz's lack of strategy and "coherent road map," but nothing happened until shareholders protested his $11 million pay package and the board got wind of their discontent. When Oracle took over, Schwartz left the company.

Hewlett-Packard got rid of Mark Hurd following a public scandal, but the company gave him such a generous severance—$28 million—that his firing appeared to be a slap on the wrist.

Now we come to the environmental disaster of the decade. Following his mismanagement of the BP oil spill, Tony Hayward was voted Worst CEO of the Year. But the board only deposed Hayward after he questioned whether BP's troubleshooters were getting ill from environmental toxins or simply had a bad case of "food poisoning." The press had a field day with this. Hayward engaged in a colossal display of whining after Deepwater Horizon dumped an estimated 200,000 gallons of oil into the Gulf of Mexico, destroying millions of fish and permanently damaging the ecosystem, by complaining that his job was too stressful and he "wanted his life back."

Restoring the Pack's Cohesiveness

What should you do when a leader has "gone bad" and is making life difficult for others?

Management consultant Mike Figliuolo has some good advice for standing up to an incompetent boss or putting a muzzle on the office bully. Figliuolo, a former honor cadet at West Point and platoon leader, knows about the proper use of power and authority.

When a boss goes off the rails, one option is direct feedback, he said. Have a talk in a neutral location and describe the behavior that you find upsetting. Dogs give each other this kind of pushback all the time: if one gets too bossy, the others rein it in with a nip or a nudge. If you're being mistreated at the office, you may need to take a similar approach.

Another option is inclusion: some people start bullying others because they feel left out. Try asking the offensive manager to join your committee or your "after hours" group to see if the situation improves, Figliuolo added.

As a last resort, there's the "professional smack down" where you gather other members of the group and accuse your boss of being unprofessional. For humans, the "full frontal assault" is generally the last resort. But not so for dogs. The pack won't hesitate to take down a bad or incompetent leader if it's clear that he no longer serves their common interests.

In recent years, too many bad managers and distracted CEOs have tarnished the reputation of American business. We'd do well to take a lesson from dogs and address aggressive or incompetent behavior early on.

PART IV

WHAT DOGS TEACH US ABOUT LIFE AND LOVE

"Man is troubled by what might be called the Dog Wish, a strange and involved compulsion to be as happy and as carefree as a dog."
—JAMES THURBER

Chapter 13

Relationship Lessons

W e've learned a lot from dogs about running healthy organizations. Now I want to talk about how dogs help us to create healthy relationships.

Over the years, my family and I have been the proud owners of three special golden retrievers: Samson, Wharf, and Dakota.

Samson joined our household about six months after Brenda and I got married. We were living in northern New Jersey, where Brenda worked at a local hospital while I commuted to my job in Manhattan and attended law school five nights a week. When Brenda was pregnant, Samson was her companion on those lonely nights when I was finishing my degree. He'd sit on the couch and rest his head on her expanding belly. Every time the baby kicked, Samson would just roll his eyes. After Rob was born, Samson slept under the crib. When we had our second son, Josh, the dog guarded him as well. Over the years, Samson looked after our boys and taught them about how to work in a partnership and share responsibility. As our boys walked him and fed him (with our supervision, of course) they learned how to be gentle, caring, and attentive. For sixteen years, Sam was their plaything, pillow, and confidant—we often heard the boys complaining to the dog whenever life with Mom and Dad had become too difficult.

Next was Wharf, a quiet dog we nicknamed "the carpet" since he could usually be found lying at our feet. Wharf was the family protector while I was on the road. He also kept Brenda sane as our teenage boys did their best to drive her crazy.

When Wharf suddenly collapsed, it seemed as if Josh, then sixteen, became an adult overnight. At the emergency veterinarian hospital, he took over and said, "My mom's too upset. Please tell me how you think we ought to handle this." Wharf had a massive inoperable tumor, so there was nothing to be done. Josh held Wharf until he died. Our dog's passing taught our boys how to cope with an unexpected loss.

Our next dog picked us. Four months later—New Year's Eve, 2000—my wife decided that we needed a new canine companion. That day, we found an ad in the local paper and went to see a breeder. As we played with the new puppies, one of them picked up Brenda's purse and headed for the door. "That must be our dog," she said.

Dakota is playful and ingenious: He learned how to give himself a massage by rolling on his ample supply of tennis balls. And he's become such a part of the family that instead of keeping him off of the sofa, we bought new furniture to match his coat.

For the past thirty-plus years, these wonderful creatures have provided us with emotional ballast and a sense of security. Brenda depended on the dogs for companionship, while I commuted to Chicago from our East Coast home. I had been offered the job at Oil-Dri, and we didn't want to move our boys while they were still in high school, so I started racking up the frequent-flier miles.

Sometimes I'd get home late on a Friday night. The family would be asleep, but Wharf and then Dakota would be at the door to greet me. I thought of the Greek warrior Odysseus, who returned home from his seafaring adventures only to be welcomed by the family dog. How does modern life compare? Our routines are more predictable and prosaic: no Sirens or Harpies, just fatigue that follows endless meetings, bad weather, delayed flights, and dealing with airport security. My dogs sat at my feet and let me unburden myself. Under their care, I transformed from a weary traveler into a family man. Through the years, my dogs have grounded me, accepted me wholeheartedly, and helped me unwind. When no one else was up, I would just talk to the dogs, confiding in them, rather than dumping all the details of each grueling week on my patient wife.

If you're a dog owner, this story will sound familiar. Nearly every one of us who has a pet talks to that animal as if it were a person. We usually start talking to our dogs as children when we desperately need to share our secret hopes and longings. These conversations continue through adulthood and often end up being among the most enduring and deeply reassuring in our lives.

Dogs understand us, and even empathize with us, but, as James Thurber might say, their genius lies in the fact that they don't talk back. Throughout the course of evolution, dogs have learned to read, recognize, and respond to our feelings and emotions. Yet, mercifully, they never developed the capacity to interrupt or offer troublesome opinions. They are wonderfully nonjudgmental. They also provide a loving presence and act as a sounding board as we face new challenges. In a way, they become a therapist for the entire family.

Freud noted that our dogs bring us a kind of clarity we have in few other relationships. The founder of psychoanalysis was recently quoted in *The Wall Street Journal* as saying, "Dogs love their friends and bite their enemies, quite unlike people, who are incapable of pure love and always have to mix love and hate in their object relations." You always know where you stand with your dog because he doesn't have the same ambivalence and conflicted feelings that we humans do. Alan Beck, who researches the human-animal bond at Purdue University, said, only half jokingly, that a dog is an ideal therapist because he listens with a cocked head and then allows you to pour out your deepest feelings, without the remotest fear of being judged. In short, we have the kind of trusting and accommodating relationship with dogs that may take years to build with people!

The Dog as the Center of the Family

Dogs, which many pet owners in the United States consider to be family members, are most likely to be found in households with children under the age of fourteen, surveys by the American Pet Products Association have found.

According to research compiled by the Center for the Human-Animal Bond at Purdue University, just having a pet in the room makes people feel safe. Dogs can also coach responses from children who are socially withdrawn or have attention deficit hyperactivity disorder, Beck told me. For this reason, many psychotherapists now bring dogs into their consulting rooms. The animal often becomes a bridge, helping these youngsters relate more easily to peers as well as adults.

Studies also show that petting a dog can affect the mood of every family member. In the process of touching the animal, we each release a powerful bonding hormone called oxytocin, bringing us into what may best be described as a state of bliss. According to Dr. Kerstin Uvnäs-Moberg, professor of physiology at the Swedish University of Agricultural Sciences, this hormone has a beneficial calming effect and is the basis for the devotion that mothers feel for their newborn children.

So forget the doghouse in the corner of the yard. The human-animal bond has shifted in the last generation. Pets have moved into the center of our domestic lives—they share our beds and have dozens of toys to amuse and distract them. In 2010, an APPA survey found that Americans spent $48.35 billion on their companion animals to keep them in a state of ease and comfort. Many Americans now put the well-being of their pets on par with their own.

Man's Best Friend as a Model of Intimacy

In my family, Samson, Dakota, and Wharf were more than creatures to be fed and pampered. They were protectors, entertainers, and loyal companions. And they were masters at engaging others. In many ways, our dogs have brought us closer to our friends and family members. When Brenda's close friend was dying of cancer, Dakota sensed her sadness, was constantly at her side, and later helped her cope with her deep sense of loss. When our neighbors' dog died, they asked if they could watch Dakota for a while, and he brought so much light and love into their house that they got another puppy. Our dogs play a key role in so many of our relationships, helping us to heal and communicate our love and concern for others.

This is what Dr. Aaron Katcher, a gifted psychoanalyst, found when he interviewed thousands of people in the 1990s about the human-animal bond for a research project at Purdue University. One of the most moving stories he and coauthor Alan Beck told in *Between Pets and People: The Importance of Animal Companionship* was about a wildlife photographer who rescued a dog injured at the scene of a car accident. The animal's paws were crushed, and he could barely move. "I named him Need," the photographer said, "because I needed him and he needed me."

The neighbors who witnessed the accident helped the photographer get the dog to a veterinarian and later raised money for his treatment. When the dog's casts were finally removed, the photographer held a party and discovered that she had a new circle of friends. Saving this animal had changed her life; she'd begun to reach out to others, and was no longer as introverted as before.

Later, the dog helped the young woman to reach out again—this time to her estranged father, a man who rarely had a kind word for anyone. When his daughter showed up with Need, he softened, and the dog became an essential link, allowing these two family members to reconnect.

A Dog for All Seasons

There's a reason animal figures show up in nursery rhymes and fairy tales in almost every culture. Children learn from animals how to behave ethically, trust their instincts, deal with survival issues, and act kindly toward other living things. In one African myth, the Creator roams the world, accompanied by his dog. In Egypt, Anubis, the Dog, is the god of the afterlife and the dispenser of justice. Sirius, the "dog star," is the brightest constellation in the night sky and an important aid to navigation. Throughout history, dogs have symbolized service, loyalty, and virtue. Animals are our moral lodestars. They have also been our wise companions at every life transition.

In early childhood, animals provide us with a sense of continuity and stability. No matter how many changes there are in the family or the home, our pets remain the same. As Alan Beck and Aaron Katcher pointed out in *Between Pets and People*, our pets allow our children "just to be" and to take a break from the constant games of winning and losing that dominate our lives. In an increasingly competitive society, children are taught to think in terms of test scores and grades, and who gets picked first for a sports team. Yet animals allow them to engage in a form of play that is collaborative and emotionally fulfilling—and has no victor.

Dogs also help our children to distinguish between the world of technology and the world of nature. They get young people away from their cell phones, video games, and computers, and remind them to stay connected with other living things.

Sociologists have known for quite a while that children who grow up to be violent criminals usually start out being cruel to animals. Researchers have recently discovered that over one-third of these young offenders have witnessed their pets being killed or beaten by family members, according to Katcher and Beck. What does this tell us? We know that the loss of a beloved pet strikes a blow against our own humanity, but the damage is even greater when the loss is caused by someone we love and trust. It's as though these children have somehow lost faith in any human connection.

Conversely, children who have been taught to nurture and care for pets tend to have more respect for others. As Beck noted in an interview, pets often serve as our first "social network." They comfort our children when they are ill or frightened, enhance their self-esteem, and serve as valued friends or confidantes. This study indicates what many of us have experienced firsthand: it's hard to feel alone if you have a dog. And in today's family, a dog can be as significant as a parent or a sibling.

"There's growing evidence, too, that interaction with animals has important implications for a child's development," Beck recently told me, "especially in the areas of social growth and communication. Pets may be the best way to teach our children how to master those difficult tasks of being more nurturing and respectful of their peers."

This is especially true for boys, he says, who have fewer models for caretaking. As the father of two boys, I can attest to this. When we went to visit my wife's family, our adult sons got down on the floor and played with all their little cousins, just as they'd played with our dogs. The family asked us how both Josh and Rob learned to be so nurturing; years later, they asked Rob to be the godfather of their youngest son.

Dogs have helped many men I know become more emotionally aware as well as more sensitive. Our dogs have taught us how to listen uncritically to friends and family members, and have shown us that we don't have to act heroic or try to fix things. All we have to do is pay attention and be present.

Good Parenting

There's one thing parents can do right, and that's to make sure their kids have a companion animal. Studies now show that children raised with pets are also likely to be healthier. Those with at least two animals are 77 percent less likely to develop allergies. And they're also less likely to suffer from nausea, diarrhea, and vomiting. In short, pets seem to have a positive effect on a child's immune system and emotional stability.

In a laboratory setting, students who spent time petting a dog had lower blood pressure and a lower heart rate, as well as lower anxiety levels. To me, this is as good an argument as any for allowing animals in schools. That's why the American Pet Products Association supports a wonderful organization, the Pet Care Trust, which promotes keeping pets in the classroom and documents the many ways they can serve as teaching aids.

Dogs can also come in handy when adults are solving problems. While your dog can't fill in your Sudoku puzzle, he can help you tackle it with greater ease. A few years ago, Dr. Karen Allen of the University at Buffalo asked three groups of young women to do some challenging math problems. One group worked alone, the second worked in the presence of their best friends, and the third was accompanied by their dogs. The results: the women who worked on the task with their dogs nearby performed dramatically better than those who worked alone or with their friends.

My sons also assure me that dogs are date magnets, and far better than any Internet matchmaking site. They're icebreakers that make it easy to approach someone on the street and start a conversation. When you first spot an attractive person, you can't easily say, "Hey! What's your name? Mind if I call you up sometime?" If you see an animal, though, you can ask, "What's your dog's name?" You'll likely receive a pleasant response that could lead to a longer conversation, perhaps about the dog's breed or how the owner got the dog. While you're talking with the owner, the dog might show off by doing some tricks. In fact, since many young people today prefer to make contact without pressure or formal expectations, engaging in banter in the dog park has become a kind of social foreplay. To encourage pet-initiated friendships to develop outside of the dog park, my son's apartment building holds a doggie social every month while wine bars in cities including New York and San Diego invite thirtysomethings to bring their canine companions to a weekly "happy hour."

Dogs and Empty Nest

Many executives interviewed for this book confessed that their dogs filled a void they experienced after their kids left home. Similarly, according to a recent survey by the American Pet Products Association, more couples are happy to have an animal to care for once their children leave the nest.

Novelist Mary Gordon confessed in *More* magazine that she missed her kids and wondered how the time passed so quickly—until she adopted a half-Lab, half-chow mix and once again heard the pitter-patter of little feet around the house. "What were the qualities I most wanted in this new dog?" she wrote. "Clearly, she needed to be a good companion. Kind, smart, loyal, entertaining. I immediately found my model: Rhoda, Mary Richards's friend on the *Mary Tyler Moore Show*."

Gordon named her dog Rhoda and was pleased when the dog learned to sit in about ten minutes and was housebroken in ten days. But after observing Rhoda run into a busy street to chase squirrels, Gordon called an obedience expert. To her surprise, she got a refresher course in parenting. "From this trainer I learned things I wish I had known when I was raising children," she wrote. "Never give a command you can't enforce. The most important thing is consistency. Don't give mixed messages."

Rhoda was "the next big relationship" in Gordon's life, but since the dog had bonded so closely to her, she began to worry about her husband. So they went to a shelter to pick out *his* companion. Of course, they wondered what they were taking on: what couple in their sixties wants to walk two dogs at night, particularly in the middle of January? The answer came easily to her: "Without kids and dogs, who can you really cuddle and how much? A cold January night is nothing like so cold as a house without non-adult creatures. Any doctor or personal trainer worth his or her salt will tell you that cuddling has been scientifically proven to contribute to a healthy heart."

In a blog for *Psychology Today* magazine, Madora Kibbe confessed to feeling a new respect for dogs after her kids left home. "I've been trying to kick a twenty-year habit of being on someone else's schedule," she wrote. "Our dogs have been my methadone. They cannot feed themselves and we don't live on a farm so they don't run wild and free. But I find them to be far more flexible than my former charges—our children. Dogs will pretty much eat whatever and wherever you feed them. They don't complain, or say, 'Ew. What's that?' Dogs don't voluntarily become vegans overnight."

A walk with her two dogs is an adventure for Kibbe. "I can take in the neighborhood," she explained, "check out the newest renovations, and see where we are in the cycle of seasons." Plus, after these excursions, she usually has something new to write about. Staying active with a dog is a way of staying active in your mind. Our dogs give us permission to explore and wander, and that's the essence of staying alert and focused, and very much alive—especially as we enter what we now call "the Third Age."

The Internet abounds with sites that recommend breeds for empty nesters. In a recent study, the American Pet Products Association found that baby boomers have a different attitude toward dogs than their parents' generation. Instead of getting rid of their pets because they're too difficult to care for, people in their sixties can't stop nurturing their animals. In short, they're addicted to caring for another living thing. We boomers also pride ourselves on remaining active, so we eagerly take on an animal's daily upkeep. As a whole, dog owners rate higher on the fitness scale and tend to stay active longer than their peers. (Take it from me: there's nothing better for our incipient aches and pains than two long walks a day and fielding lots of tennis balls.)

Better Senior Moments

Dogs can also help us deal creatively with our much older parents. When my wife, Brenda, was growing up, animals were an integral part of her home life. Her mother adopted several cats and at least five dogs, as well as wounded birds, peacocks, ducks, chickens, rats, lizards, and snakes. The three chinchillas they saved from slaughter multiplied to a dozen; soon the house and yard began to resemble Noah's ark. Having animals clearly helped Brenda's parents stay young. This Christmas we coaxed my ninety-five-year-old father into playing with my son's bulldog, Percy, and I was thrilled when he responded to the little dog's energy, getting up from his armchair a little more often than usual, and exercising his arms by playing tug with the dog. By the end of our visit, Dad was sitting contentedly with Percy on his lap, just quietly petting him.

Dogs are soothing for our elders because, as Brenda puts it, petting them puts us into a kind of trance. Our pets have been moving from the backyard to the bedroom for a reason; they're a wonderful source of intimacy and may be the only source of touch for older people, who often spend much of their time alone. "The Pet Connection," as my friend Dr. Marty Becker calls it, seems to have a magical effect on our mood and on our health. These benefits are even more important as we age. According to Dr. Edward Creagan, an oncologist at the Mayo Clinic in Rochester, Minnesota, seniors with pets have 21 percent fewer visits to the doctor, along with lower blood pressure and better coping skills.

Dr. Rebecca Johnson, of the Center of Excellence on Aging at the University of Missouri, found that people who spend quiet time with a dog also have high levels of serotonin, the body's own "feel-good" chemical. This is one way to treat the depression so common among the elderly. Doctors like Edward Creagan are already handing out prescriptions for a pooch instead of Prozac, and I'll bet we see more contented older folks as more physicians learn about the physical and psychological benefits of dogs.

Patients with aggressive Alzheimer's disease were helped by the presence of a therapy dog, according to a 1999 study by researchers at the University of Nebraska Medical Center College of Nursing, while a study by researchers at the University of Kentucky College of Medicine indicated that pet owners cope better with the loss of a loved one.

"A pet is a medication without side effects," the Mayo Clinic's Creagan told *USA Weekend*. "I can't always explain it...but for years now I've seen how instances of having a pet is like an effective drug. It really does help people." This is an area the American Pet Products Association intends to explore with the Human-Animal Bond Research Initiative, created in partnership with Purdue University. This bond is so strong and so deeply etched into our biology that it may turn out to be one of our best and most effective medicines.

How Dogs Give Us Staying Power

Having a dog may also, to some degree, determine how long and how well we live. Dr. Karen Allen's research indicated that dogs help people with high-pressure jobs relax and lower their stress levels. Thus pet ownership can be a "preventive health measure" for Type A executives. Similarly, a team of researchers in Australia found that people with pets had lower blood fat levels (cholesterol and triglycerides) and lower blood pressure than those without companion animals.

We now have a long list of the ways that we can benefit from spending time with dogs. Dogs teach us to be eloquent observers of people's feelings and emotions. They remind us to be kind, observant, and sensitive. They are a loving and stabilizing force in families. They make us healthier, happier, and stronger. They help us cope with stress and change. They teach us about loyalty and service, and wholehearted acceptance of those we love. What better partners can we have at any age?

Chapter 14

Generosity and Giving Back

For the past eight years, I've been a supporter of Green Chimneys, a farm in Brewster, New York, that helps children with learning disabilities as well as emotional and behavioral problems. Each year hundreds of grade-schoolers come to this special place from New York City, northern New York, and western Connecticut to work with animals and learn how to be responsible caretakers. They leave with a new sense of their own worth and the faith that they can make the world a better place. While not as well known, Green Chimneys served as the inspiration for Paul Newman's Hole in the Wall Camp.

Richard Gere, Hillary Clinton, Martha Stewart, Vanessa Williams, and Desmond Tutu have all helped to expand this program. Those of us who volunteer see firsthand the tremendous healing effect that animals have on children. The work I do with Green Chimneys is among the most rewarding things I've done, and I've learned a good deal from the farm's octogenarian founder, Samuel Ross, about how contact with nature can turn children into natural leaders.

Raised in the Hotel Roosevelt in New York City, the young Sam Ross never went anywhere without his dog. In his mind, animals were forever linked to a sense of adventure and exploration, and to the learning process. That's the whole reason he built Green Chimneys and created a whole new form of education, more than sixty years ago, when he himself was barely out of school.

At the age of fourteen, Ross headed off to the University of Montreal to study French. On the long drive north, he and his father planned to deliver some Ovaltine to a young friend at a boarding school upstate.

When they arrived, "the door opened," Ross recalled, "and I saw a meagerly set dining table without enough food for the kids. In the hallway was a mosaic of Ovaltine cans that had never been opened." Right then he told his father, "I know what I want to do. I want to open a school for very young children on a farm so everyone can eat well and have a healthy life."

"What do you know about schools?" his father asked.

"Well, I've been in them all my life," the young Ross replied.

A year later, his father bought Green Chimneys Farm, encompassing seventy-five acres, for $38,500. When Ross finished his undergraduate degree at age seventeen, he began his life's goal of launching the Green Chimneys School for Little Folk.

"Our first year, 1948, we ran a summer camp," Ross recalled, "then we added the word 'school' to get approval from the Department of Education. Our original plan was to produce our food and be very self-sufficient."

Green Chimneys started off with 5,000 chickens, some Jersey cows, and a few goats and sheep. The kids bonded immediately to the animals, prompting Ross to pledge to keep the animals at the farm for their natural lifetime. Today, when children return to the farm to see the animals that they've helped raise, it "gives them a sense of continuity and reminds many of them of that first moment when they felt they had an important job to do," Ross said.

Ross intuitively knew that animals could serve as a stabilizing force for children and families, years before we had studies to prove it. When Green Chimneys turned into a full-fledged school, it began accepting kids who had learning disabilities, who lived in foster homes, or who were at risk of becoming juvenile delinquents

Green Chimneys, which is open 24/7, has 210 official school days—thirty more than public schools. It's still run by Ross, who now has advanced degrees in psychology, education, and administration. "These children need more attention than the public schools can give them," he said. "A lot of them are playing catch-up. They don't need more rote learning; they need a total living experience. Our program includes nature-based studies, care of wildlife, a therapeutic riding program, horticulture in the greenhouse and in the garden, and animal-assisted learning." These children also have the opportunity to train service dogs for the blind and disabled through the East Coast

Assistance Dogs program at Green Chimneys. When veterans come to Green Chimneys, some in wheelchairs, the kids show them what the dogs can do.

Several children who board there today were adopted from Russia, but didn't adjust to their new families. Others have had difficulty maintaining friendships or getting along with their siblings. But Ross has figured out a way to help them develop stable relationships.

"When children first come to Green Chimneys, they're paired off with a companion animal so right away, they make a friend," Ross said. "By caring for that animal, the children learn responsibility and consistency. They also learn how to trust and eventually become more open with the counselors and their peers."

"People say animals provide unconditional love," Ross told me. "But that's not true. It's a reciprocal arrangement. Our children learn very early on, if you are nice to the animals, they will be nice to you. They also discover that accidents occur when our creatures are afraid or startled. It's the same with human beings." His goal is for the children to become more sensitive to others, more aware of others, and more observant of the world around them. For that purpose, the farm is an ideal teaching tool.

Green Chimneys is a special learning environment. Knock on a classroom door and it may be opened by a dog! Students also spend a good portion of each day outdoors, working with animals or plants in the greenhouse or the fields. They learn the importance of their labors when they gather eggs laid by the chickens and harvest vegetables grown on the farm—which are used to feed local communities—and when wool from the sheep and goats is turned into beautiful yarn. Ross knows that nature is our primary teacher, and that caring for animals instills the habit of nurturing and taking care of others. That's why his pioneering program accomplishes so much: It mends broken lives. It gives children new hope and confidence and instructs them in the art of giving back.

It doesn't matter what job these young people start out doing—it's the sense of being useful that's so transformative. I'll never forget one young boy whose job it was to clean out the kennels. He said, "Because of me, these dogs have a good life." When he looked at me, I could see the hope and the growing self-esteem in his eyes.

How Dogs Teach Us Generosity

We used to say, "It's a dog's life," referring to one of Dickensian misery. Yet this expression has a different meaning in America today. A dog's life is now one of loyalty and devotion. My sister-in-law suffered a stroke in her backyard and lay outdoors for two days in fifty-five-degree weather. Yet her dog, Darcy, lay on top of her the whole time keeping her warm. The doctors said she would have died from exposure had it not been for the dog's swift, instinctive response.

Since the first human settlements appeared on earth, dogs have been our most trusted helpmates.

Dogs have rescued us from earthquakes and disasters, comforted the elderly, helped autistic children, assisted the blind and disabled. They've entered hospitals, therapy rooms, courtrooms, and classrooms. Dogs have also made countless contributions to our well-being.

At every step of the way, dogs have helped us deepen our own capacity for giving. Why? Dogs always give more than they get. As we follow their example, we find it easier to open up our hearts and be more generous with our resources.

Many of the dog-owning CEOs I know embody this altruism. Consider Bruce FaBrizio, founder, CEO, and president of Sunshine Makers, a company that sells environmentally safe cleaning products under the label Simple Green. FaBrizio takes a dog's innate willingness to please as the model for his EGBAR Foundation (EGBAR stands for "Everything's Gonna Be All Right"). He said that this is how he has felt, "with one golden retriever after the other riding shotgun at my company for the past thirty-give years."

The EGBAR Foundation educates children throughout the world about the importance of recycling and protecting the environment. It reaches out to schools to build greater awareness of our environmental cleanup needs with projects focusing on beaches, forests, and cities. And it shows all members of the community, both young and old, how they can "make a difference" and leave this world in better shape.

APPA, too, is doing its part to give back on a variety of levels. We sponsor Green Chimneys and provide pet supplies for those in need during natural disasters like Hurricane Katrina and Japan's tsunami-earthquake. We recently partnered with Purdue University to create the Human-Animal Bond Research Initiative. And we're constantly exploring the ways dogs and other animals make us healthier and happier—and contribute to our work and family lives.

Generation X is of particular interest because young people have a doglike generosity in their commitment to building strong communities and creating a healthier environment.

As Donna Fenn reported in her book *Upstarts*, young people today are more interested in doing good and in creating new business models that combine nonprofit and for-profit ventures, tackling everything from education to alternative energy. In *Upstarts*, she profiles Bill Downing, who has a canine generosity of spirit. Downing cofounded two education companies with his high school guidance counselor, Rick Singer, and now provides tutoring and college coaching to students in sixty cities, including Tokyo, London, and Hong Kong. Downing has also put some of his profits into helping high school athletes in low-income communities bring up their grade point averages. "Anyone can work with rich kids," Downing said, "but what about the kid in East Palo Alto who's got nothing?"

Rajiv Kumar, another entrepreneur described in *Upstarts*, showed his concern for the pack when he founded Shape Up the Nation as a first-year medical student at Brown University. Shape Up now manages employee wellness programs for clients including Medtronic and the Cleveland Clinic, and also runs statewide wellness competitions to educate people about fitness and preventive care. "Our not-for-profit is our way of thinking globally and acting locally," Kumar said. "It's fulfilling our design to bring about change in the world."

Similarly, Google, one of the first Silicon Valley high-tech companies to let dogs wander freely through the hallways, is now supporting renewable energy alternatives and tracking the condition of the world's forests, while it's big brother to the north, Microsoft, is spearheading global health initiatives and tackling disease in poverty-ridden countries.

Generosity is good for us. It's a quality that's been linked to better physical and emotional health. People who give back are rewarded with a sense of meaning and purpose, and as leaders, they are capable of drawing on the friendship and loyalty of others. Over the years I've found that people who have dogs or other companion animals tend to feel more connected to the world at large, and more responsible for its well-being.

My dog Dakota embodies the four qualities associated with generous people. Simply put, a dog is a fine example of:

- Altruism—giving with no thought of reward or compensation, but from an eagerness to help.
- Optimism—the sense that something wonderful is always just about to happen.

- Trust—a willingness to follow those we love and come to their aid in difficult situations.
- Energy—a sense of vitality and the ability to engage others.

Generous people show an eagerness to get involved and have a rare ability to bring others along with their infectious enthusiasm. These are traits we associate with leadership and that we find in increasing abundance in Generations X and Y.

How Dogs Help Us Build Community

Dogs don't just remind us to be generous; they also function as a kind of social glue. In fact, researchers in Australia found that pets have a ripple effect, helping us connect with ourselves and enhancing our sense of community. Man's best friend is a social facilitator, encouraging us to be friendly and chat with people we meet in the park or the dog run. Busy CEOs, working parents, and retired people—all are short on time for socializing and welcome the opportunity to make new friends as they take Rover for a stroll. Pets are also a catalyst for reciprocity. You might say to your neighbor, "You take Max while we're on vacation, and when you're out of town, we'll babysit Darcy." Dogs provide us with opportunities for mutual caretaking and help us establish bonds with neighbors.

Dog ownership is linked to increased civic engagement, neighborhood patrols, cleanup committees, and efforts to restore local parks. The reason is simple: when you're out and about with your dog, you notice things that need fixing. You're more aware of your neighbors' habits and activities. And you're more tuned into the community as a whole. No wonder the same Australian researchers reported that dog owners feel safer and have a stronger sense of belonging than those living without companion animals.

We also live in an age of constant change—people often move, change jobs, and switch schools. The impersonal nature of our cities and our suburbs gives rise to a sense of estrangement, and many of us feel cut off from our roots. Yet dogs help to get us up close and personal with our neighbors, and, as we walk with them, we discover what's so special about where we live. Dogs bring us out into nature, where we can watch the changes in the light and the passing of the seasons. They give us an excuse to simply stand there, looking up at the night sky, considering our place among the stars.

There's no end to the benefits we derive from our canine companions. But here are the ones that come to mind most often. My dog is the ultimate connector. He takes me on adventures. He provides the crazy, lighthearted stories I share with my children and my friends. He makes me laugh and reminds me to see to it that others are happy and well cared for. In more than thirty years in the business world, I have found no better model for generosity and openheartedness. The motto that I live by is simple—strive to be as good a person as my dog thinks I am.

Chapter Notes

INTRODUCTION: MY DOG IS MY CEO

PAGE 1

According to an informal poll: Del Jones, "Dog Loving CEOs Have a Few Tips for the Obamas and Bo," *USA Today*, April 17, 2009, http://www.usatoday.com/money/companies/management/2009-04-13-CEO-dog-tips-obamas_N.htm.

PAGE 2

Canis familiaris *appeared on the scene*: Alan Beck (director, Center for the Human-Animal Bond, Purdue University School of Veterinary Medicine), in discussion with the author, September 2010. (This estimate is used by many researchers, including Beck. Also see Tim Wogan's article, "Small Dogs Evolved in Middle East," in *Science*NOW, February 24, 2010, http://news.sciencemag.org/sciencenow/2010/02/small-dogs-evolved-in-middle-eas.html.)

PAGE 3

"I would love to have the intuition": Del Jones, "Dog Loving CEOs Have a Few Tips for the Obamas and Bo" (includes an interview with Dave Young), *USA Today*.

"Never work with someone": "Dog Loving CEOs Have a Few Tips for the Obamas and Bo" (includes an interview with Ben Golub), *USA Today*.

PAGE 5

British scientist Rupert Sheldrake: Rupert Sheldrake, *Dogs That Know When Their Owners Are Coming Home* (New York: Three Rivers Press, 2000).

neuropsychologist Stanley Coren: Stanley Coren, "How Dogs Read Human Body Language," *Modern Dog*, http://www.moderndogmagazine.com/articles/how-dogs-read-human-body-language/278.

CHAPTER 1: THE CANINE CONNECTION

http://www.pbs.org/wgbh/nova/nature/dogs-decoded.html.

PAGE 16

According to a study by Dr. Albert Mehrabian: Albert Mehrabian, *Silent Messages: A Wealth of Information About Nonverbal Communication* (Belmont, CA: Wadsworth, 1971).

> For further information, see Albert Mehrabian and Susan R. Ferris, "Inference of Attitudes from Nonverbal Communication in Two Channels," *Journal of Consulting Psychology*, vol. 31, no. 3 (June 1967): 248–58. Also see Albert Mehrabian, *Nonverbal Communication* (Chicago: Aldine-Atherton, 1972).

PAGE 19

"We learned how significant": Elizabeth Kirkhart (cofounder, Moving Boundaries), in discussion with the author, November 2009.

PAGE 20

It's a truism that: C.J. Prince, "Are You Blind to the Truth?" October 2010, http://chiefexecutive.net/are-you-blind-to-the-truth.

PAGE 22

Omar Hamoui, former CEO: Adam Bryant, Corner Office: Omar Hamoui, *New York Times*, May 1, 2010, http://www.nytimes.com/2010/05/02/business/02corner.html.

PAGE 24

"We don't punish": Susan Tripp (founder, Animal Behavior Network), in discussion with the author, September 2009.

PAGE 25

When Joseph Plumeri: Adam Bryant, Corner Office: Joseph Plumeri, *New York Times*, December 5, 2009, http://www.nytimes.com/2009/12/06/business/06corner.html.

Mindy Grossman, CEO of retailer HSN: Adam Bryant, Corner Office: Mindy Grossman, *New York Times*, November 14, 2009, http://www.nytimes.com/2009/11/15/business/15corner.html.

PAGE 26

Then there's Jeffrey Katzenberg: Adam Bryant, Corner Office: Jeffrey Katzenberg, *New York Times*, November 7, 2009, http://www.nytimes.com/2009/11/08/business/08corner.html.

PAGE 28

"We have assumed that there's a single animal": Beck, discussion.

PAGE 29

"I was once a command-and-control guy": Adam Bryant, Corner Office: Joseph Plumeri.

William Green, chairman and: Adam Bryant, Corner Office: William Green, *New York Times*, November 21, 2009, http://www.nytimes.com/2009/11/22/business/22corner.html.

PAGE 30

A report by the Institute for the Future: "American Knowledge Worker Across the Generations: Eight Dynamic Dimensions,"

Institute for the Future, December 2001, http://www.iftf.org/node/919.

PAGE 33

The American anthropologist Elizabeth Marshall Thomas: Elizabeth Marshall Thomas, *The Social Lives of Dogs* (New York: Pocketbooks, 2000), 212.

Pascal was in line to take the top position: Tim Arango, "Sony's Version of Tracy and Hepburn," *New York Times*, October 24, 2009, http://www.nytimes.com/2009/10/25/business/media/25sony.html.

PAGE 34

To survive, Sony chairman Howard Stringer: Tim Arango, "Sony's Version of Tracy and Hepburn" (includes an interview with Howard Stringer), *New York Times*.

PAGE 36

"This practice started": W. Stanton Smith (former principal, Deloitte & Touche), in discussion with the author, September 2009.

PAGE 38

The trouble is, as companies keep downsizing: Sarah Anderson, Chuck Collins, Sam Pizzigati, and Kevin Shih, "CEO Pay and the Great Recession," the Institute for Policy Studies, September 1, 2010, http://www.ips-dc.org/reports/executive_excess_2010.

PAGE 40

In 2006, economist Sylvia Ann Hewlett: Sylvia Ann Hewlett, "Making Flex Time a Win-Win," *New York Times*, December 12, 2009, http://www.nytimes.com/2009/12/13/jobs/13pre.html.

PAGE 41

Members of Generation Y are willing to work 24/7: "American Knowledge Workers Across the Generations," Institute for the Future.

PAGE 42

Verlyn Klinkenborg, writing in The New York Times: Verlyn Klinkenborg, "Why Do Sled Dogs Run?" *New York Times*, February 13, 2010, http://www.nytimes.com/2010/02/14/opinion/14sun2.html.

Fred Seddequi, CEO of Silicon Valley Venture Partners: Fred Seddequi (CEO, Silicon Valley Venture Partners), in discussion with the author, August 2009.

PAGE 43

Jeff Swartz, president and CEO: Adam Bryant, Corner Office: Jeff Swartz, *New York Times*, December 19, 2009, http://www.nytimes.com/2009/12/20/business/20corner.html.

CHAPTER 2: WHAT BREED OF MANAGER ARE YOU?

PAGE 63

"I say no to him": Damon Kitney, "Secret to Virgin's Success: Saying No to Dr. Yes" (includes an interview with Stephen Murphy), *Australian*, November 13, 2010, http://www.theaustralian.com.au/business/secret-to-virgins-success-saying-no-to-dr-yes/story-e6frg8zx-1225952874484.

PAGE 65

"Leaders like this": Kermit Pattison, "What Breed Is Your CEO? Randy Komisar on Leadership and Management," *Fast Company*, July 27, 2010, http://www.fastcompany.com/1674779/randy-komisar-kleiner-perkins-caufield-byer-leadership-management-entrepreneurship.

CHAPTER 3: WHY THE PACK MENTALITY IS GOOD FOR BUSINESS

PAGE 69

Studies show that the chief reason: "Workers Agree: Company Culture Matters" Randstad US and Ipsos Public Affairs, October 4, 2010, http://us.randstad.com/content/aboutrandstad/news-and-press-releases/press-releases/2010/20101004005.xml.

"Most managers look at personal conversations": Wallace Immen, "Water Cooler Chats Can Raise Productivity" (includes an interview with Charlice Hurst),*Globe and Mail*, November 2, 2010, available online to subscribers.

PAGE 70

"When I first started out": Smith, discussion.

"What Makes the Job Tough: The Influence of Organizational Respect on Burnout in the Human Services," by Lakshmi Ramarajan and Sigal Barsade, the Wharton School of Business, http://knowledge.wharton.upenn.edu/papers/1327.pdf.

PAGES 70–71

A recent study by Hewitt Associates: Courtney Rubin, "Why Happy Employees are Good for Business," *Inc.*, September 20, 2010, http://www.inc.com/news/articles/2010/09/happy-employees-are-good-for-business.html.

PAGE 71

"because they are friendlier": Robin Koval (president, Kaplan Thaler Group), in discussion with the author, February 2010.

PAGE 73

This doglike empathy: Linda Tischler, "IDEO's David Kelley on 'Design Thinking,'" *Fast Company*, February 1, 2009, http://www.fastcompany.com/magazine/132/a-designer-takes-on-his-biggest-challenge-ever.html.

PAGE 74

As he recounts in Delivering Happiness: Tony Hsieh, *Delivering Happiness: A Path to Profits, Passion, and Purpose* (New York: Business Plus, 2010), 146.

PAGE 75

The Ritz-Carlton shows: Robert Reiss, "How Ritz-Carlton Stays at the Top: An Interview with Simon F. Cooper, President of the Ritz-Carlton Company," *Forbes*, October 30, 2009, http://www.forbes.com/2009/10/30/simon-cooper-ritz-leadership-ceonetwork-hotels.html.

CHAPTER 4: CULTIVATE A CANINE
SENSE OF PLAY

PAGE 84

The best of all leaders: Tony Schwartz, "The Four Capacities Every Great Leader Needs (and Very Few Have)," *Harvard Business Review* (blog), October 13, 2010, http://blogs.hbr.org/cgi-bin/mt/mt-tb.cgi/8210.

PAGE 86

"Fun is one of the important": Adam Bryant, Corner Office: Niki Leondakis, *New York Times*, June 12, 2010, http://www.nytimes.com/2010/06/13/business/13corner.html.

Humor, on the other hand: David Abramis, "Humor in Healthy Organizations," *HR Magazine*, vol. 7, no. 8 (August 1992): 74.

PAGE 87

According to a study by American Express: Justin Ewers, "All Work and No Play Makes a Company...Unproductive," *U.S. News & World Report*, August 5, 2007, http://www.usnews.com/usnews/biztech/articles/070805/13smallbiz.htm.

PAGE 90

But boredom ranks up at the top: Charles Wallace, "Workers in the Recession: Stress, Boredom and Too Little Pay," *Daily Finance*, September 10, 2010, http://www.dailyfinance.com/2010/09/10/workers-recession-stress-boredom-and-too-little-pay/.

The companies named by Entrepreneur: "The Top Small & Medium Companies to Work for 2010," *Entrepreneur*, 2010, www.entrepreneur.com/greatplaces/.

PAGE 92

the Phelps Group: Matthew Fogel, "Offsite Bloopers: What Could Possibly Go Wrong at the Annual Summer Outing?" *Inc.*, June 1, 2003, http://www.inc.com/magazine/20030601/25518.html.

Cynthia McKay, CEO of Le Gourmet: "Offsite Bloopers: What Could Possibly Go Wrong at the Annual Summer Outing?" (includes an interview with Cynthia McKay), *Inc.*

PAGE 93

"It's a break for us": Lorraine Mirabella, "Improving Staff Morale Can Be Like Child's Play" (includes an interview with Lucy Rermgosakul), *Baltimore Sun*, March 21, 2001, http://articles.baltimoresun.com/2010-03-21/business/bal-bz.moonbounce21mar21_1_morale-team-building-workers.

One in four American workers: "All Work and No Play Makes a Company . . . Unproductive," *U.S. News & World Report*.

CHAPTER 5: FOSTER DOGGED INNOVATION

PAGE 97

At Stanford University's Graduate School of Business: Curtis Sittenfeld, "The Most Creative Man in Silicon Valley," *Fast Company*, May 31, 2000, http://www.fastcompany.com/magazine/35/ray.html.

PAGE 99

Bob Moog, president of University Games: "The Most Creative Man in Silicon Valley" (includes an interview with Bob Moog), *Fast Company*.

PAGE 100

"If the group is larger": Smith, discussion.

"Go beyond seven people": Bill Scudder (vice president and chief information officer, Sonus Networks), in discussion with the author, September 2010.

Entrepreneur Fred Seddiqui: Seddiqui, discussion.

PAGES 100–101

Researchers have also found that: Omar A. Alnuaimi, Lionel P. Robert, Jr., and Likoebe M. Maruping, "Team Size, Dispersion, and Social Loafing in Technology-Supported Teams: A Perspective on the Theory of Moral Disengagement," *Journal of Management Information Systems*, vol. 27, no. 1 (Summer 2010): 203–230.

PAGE 101

The "pack principle" applies on Madison Avenue: Koval, discussion.

No one has embraced the pack mentality: Donna Fenn (author, *Upstarts! How GenY Entrepreneurs Are Rocking the World of Business and 8 Ways You Can Profit from Their Success*), in discussion with the author, October 2010.

PAGE 102

Researchers at Carnegie Mellon: "New Study by Carnegie Mellon, MIT and Union College Shows Collective Intelligence of Groups Exceeds Cognitive Abilities of Individual Group Members," October 1, 2010, http://www.cmu.edu/news/archive/2010/October/oct1_collectiveintelligencestudy.shtml.

PAGE 103
When Bob Moog founded University Games: "The Most Creative Man in Silicon Valley," *Fast Company*.

PAGE 106
In 2010, Inc. magazine's website: World's Coolest Offices," *Inc.*, http://www.inc.com/worlds-coolest-offices-2010/index.html.

CHAPTER 6: BRING FIDO TO WORK

PAGE 107
many people live two lives: Liz Palika and Jennifer Fearing, *Dogs at Work: A Practical Guide to Creating Dog-Friendly Workplaces* (Washington, DC: Humane Society Press, 2008).

PAGE 108
"Having dogs in the workplace": Jeanine Falcon (human resources director, Replacements) in discussion with the author, September 2010.

PAGE 109
When dogs visit the headquarters: Carol Chapin (vice president of research and development, Sunshine Makers), in discussion with the author, September 2010.

PAGE 111
Karen Allen, a research associate professor: Karen Allen, Barbara E. Shykoff, and Joseph L. Izzo, Jr., "Pet Ownership, but Not ACE Inhibitor Therapy, Blunts Home Blood Pressure Responses to Mental Stress," *Hypertension* (October 2001): 815–20, www.acsu.buffalo.edu/~kmallen/AllenPet.pdf.

PAGE 112
increase our levels of oxytocin: Miho Nagasawa, Takefumi Kikusui, Tatsushi Onaka, and Mitsuaki Ohta, "Dog's Gaze at

Its Owner Increases Owner's Urinary Oxytocin During Social Interaction," *Hormones and Behavior*, vol. 55, no. 3 (March 2009): 434–41, www.univie.ac.at/mcogneu/lit/nagasawa. pdf. Also see transcript of *Dogs Decoded*, PBS, http://www.pbs.org/wgbh/nova/nature/dogs-decoded.html, which includes research by Kerstin Uvnäs-Moberg of the Karolinska Institute in Sweden.

PAGE 112

The American Pet Products Association: "Win Over Your Boss with these Dog Day Facts," 2006, www.takeyourdog.com/Get-Involved/win-over-your-boss.php.

CHAPTER 7: REWARD IN REAL TIME

PAGE 117

Yahoo's CEO, Carol Bartz: Adam Bryant, Corner Office: Carol Bartz, *New York Times*, October 17, 2009, http://www.nytimes.com/2009/10/18/business/18corner.html.

PAGE 118

"Our story is a lot like Microsoft's": Kathy Clinton (human resources director, Autodesk), in discussion with the author, October 2010.

Greger Larson, an archaeologist at Durham University: Nova: Dogs Decoded, PBS.

PAGE 120

"When you give less than 5 percent": Mike Figliuolo (founder and managing director of *thoughtLEADERS*), in discussion with the author, September 2010.

PAGE 124

"Our people are highly altruistic": Zeev Neuwirth (chief officer of clinical effectiveness and innovation, Harvard Vanguard Health), in discussion with the author, September 2010.

Netflix founder Reed Hastings: Robert J. Grossman, "Tough Love at Netflix," *HR Magazine*, vol. 55., no. 4 (April 1, 2010), available online to subscribers.

PAGE 125

"The advantages of trusting people": "Tough Love at Netflix" (includes an interview with Patty McCord), *HR Magazine*.

"When we ask people why": "Tough Love at Netflix" (includes an interview with Allison Hopkins), *HR Magazine*.

PAGE 126

In a later study, Adam Grant: Adam Grant and Devin T. Mathias, "Recruiting and Motivating Fundraising Callers: How Making a Difference…Makes a Difference," http://moredonors.com/motivating.pdf.

Zappos founder Tony Hsieh: Hsieh, *Delivering Happiness*, 162.

PAGE 127

According to a 2009 survey: Joe Walker, "Even with a Recovery, Job Perks May Not Return," *Wall Street Journal*, April 5, 2010, http://online.wsj.com/article/SB10001424052702304017404575165854181296256.html. Also see "2009 Employee Benefits," Society for Human Resource Management (2009), http://www.shrm.org/Research/SurveyFindings/Articles/Documents/09-0295_Employee_Benefits_Survey_Report_spread_fnl.pdf.

"Benefits come back slowly": "Even with a Recovery, Job Perks May Not Return" (includes an interview with Peter Cappelli), *Wall Street Journal*.

PAGE 128

America's top CEOs: "100 Best Companies to Work For," *Fortune*, February 7, 2011, http://money.cnn.com/magazines/fortune/bestcompanies/2011/index.html.

PAGE 129

"Firms that 'get it'": Steve Arneson (president, Arneson Leadership Consulting), in discussion with the author, April 2010.

Pitney Bowes prides itself: Matt Broder (chief information officer, Pitney Bowes), in discussion with the author, October 2010.

PAGE 130

As Businessweek reported, IBM a few years ago: Jena McGregor, Michael Arndt, Robert Berner, Ian Rowley, Kenji Hall, Gail Edmondson, Steve Hamm, Moon Ihlwan, and Andy Reinhardt, "The World's Most Innovative Companies," *Businessweek*, April 24, 2006, http://www.businessweek.com/magazine/content/06_17/b3981401.htm.

PAGE 131

Members of Generation Y seem to be: Fenn, discussion.

CHAPTER 8: CORRECT EARLY

PAGE 134

In a survey of human resources professionals: "The State of Performance Management," WorldatWork and Sibson Consulting, July 2007, www.worldatwork.org/waw/adimLink?id=20261.

In fact, Samuel Culbert: Tara Parker-Pope, "Time to Review Workplace Reviews?" (includes an interview with Samuel Culbert), *New York Times* (blog: "The Well"), May 17, 2010, http://well.blogs.nytimes.com/2010/05/17/time-to-review-workplace-reviews/.

In Get Rid of the Performance Review! Samuel Culbert and Lawrence Rout, *Get Rid of the Performance Review! How*

Companies Can Stop Intimidating, Start Managing—and Focus on What Really Matters (New York: Business Plus, 2010).

PAGE 135

Receiving timely feedback is critical: Marguerite M. Callaway (founder and president, the Callaway Leadership Institute), in discussion with the author, September 2010.

PAGE 137

But according to Clifford Nass: Bruna Martinuzzi, "The Criticism Sandwich: A Stale Idea," Clarion Enterprises (blog), December 21, 2010, http://www.clarionenterprises. com/blog/index.php?s=criticism+sandwich.

CHAPTER 9: STAY ON MESSAGE

PAGE 139

"Dogs like to know": Tripp, discussion.

These firms, which have appeared: "100 Best Companies to Work For," *Fortune*.

PAGE 140

W. L. Gore…assembled: "100 Best Companies to Work For," *Fortune*.

Although the company sells china: Falcon, discussion.

PAGE 141

When Zappos founder Tony Hsieh: Hsieh, *Delivering Happiness*, 94.

A report by Gallup: "State of the American Workplace: 2008-2010," Gallup Consulting, 2010, http://www.gallup.com/con-sulting/142724/state-american-workplace-2008-2010.aspx.

PAGE 142

Aylwin B. Lewis: "At Sears, A Great Communicator," *Businessweek*, October 31, 2005, http://www.businessweek. com/magazine/content/05_44/b3957103.htm.

PAGE 144

A few years ago, workers at Molson Coors: Miri Zena MacDonald, "How Molson Coors Brewed Up Stronger Engagement," *SmartBlog on Workforce*, November 12, 2010, http://smartblogs.com/leadership/2010/11/12/how-molson-coors-brewed-up-stronger-engagement/.

PAGE 145

Sunshine Makers, which produces: Denise Dochnahl (marketing specialist, Sunshine Makers), in discussion with the author, September 2010.

PAGE 147

"Dogs are always trying": Tripp, discussion.

CHAPTER 10: LEAD BY EXAMPLE

PAGE 149

"The most frequent complaints": Judith Brown, "Employee Orientation: Keeping New Employees on Board," About. com, accessed May 25, 2011, http://humanresources.about. com/od/retention/a/keepnewemployee.htm.

PAGE 153

"If you go back": Peter Cappelli, "Workplace Loyalties Change but the Value of Mentoring Doesn't," Wharton School of Business (blog), May 16, 2007, http://knowledge.wharton. upenn.edu/article.cfm?articleid=1736.

PAGE 155

A five-year study at Sun Microsystems: "Workplace Loyalties Change but the Value of Mentoring Doesn't," Wharton School of Business (blog).

Intel is taking a fresh approach: Fara Warner, "Inside Intel's Mentoring Movement," *Fast Company*, March 31, 2002, http://www.fastcompany.com/magazine/57/chalktalk.html.

PAGE 156

Harris Bank takes a similar approach: Glen Fest, "Top Team: Executive Class at Harris Bank" (includes an interview with Deirdre Drake), *U.S. Banker*, October 2010, http://www.americanbanker.com/usb_issues/120_10/executive-class-1026095-1.html.
Deloitte & Touche, a global: Smith, discussion.

PAGE 157

"I wanted a puppy": Robert Reiss, "A CEO from the Age of 5: An Interview with Murray Martin, chief executive officer of Pitney Bowes," *Forbes*, November 11, 2010, http://www.forbes.com/2010/11/01/murray-martin-pitney-bowes-leadership-managing-interview.html.

PAGE 158

It takes anywhere from eight to ten weeks: R. Williams "Mellon Learning Curve Research Study," Mellon Financial Corp., 2003, http://www.shrm.org/Research/Articles/Articles/Pages/OrganizationalEntryOnboarding,OrientationAndSocialization.aspx.

CHAPTER 11: ENCOURAGE INTELLIGENT DISOBEDIENCE

PAGE 165

"today's leaders get little training": Arneson, discussion. Also see Steve Arneson, *Bootstrap Leadership: 50 Ways to Break Out,*

Take Charge, and Move Up (San Francisco: Berrett-Koehler Publishers, 2010).

PAGE 166

in 2010, the company announced: "Wal-Mart Unveils Global Sustainable Agriculture Goals," Wal-Mart, October 14, 2010, http://walmartstores.com/pressroom/news/10376.aspx.

PAGE 167

Leadership expert Bruna Martinuzzi: Bruna Martinuzzi, "The Art of Intelligent Disobedience," Clarion Enterprises (blog), May 19, 2010, http://www.clarionenterprises.com/blog/index.php?s=disobedience.

PAGE 169

ESI International: Robert McGannon, "The Difference Between Good and Great Project Managers," Project Smart. co.uk, accessed May 25, 2011, http://www.projectsmart. co.uk/difference-between-good-and-great-project-managers. html.

PAGE 170

Debra Tosch, executive director: Debra Tosch (executive director, Search Dog Foundation), in discussion with the author, October 2010.

CHAPTER 12: BAD DOG, BAD HIRE

PAGE 178

When we fail to find a good fit: F. John Reh, "What Good People Really Cost," About.com, accessed May 25, 2011, http://management.about.com/cs/people/a/WhatPeopleCost.htm.

PAGE 181

Employees complained anonymously: "Low-Quality Management," unidentified Sun Microsystems systems engineer, current employee, comment on Glassdoor.com, June 30, 2009, http://www.glassdoor.com/GD/Reviews/Sun-Microsystems-Reviews-E1924.htm?filter.jobTitleFTS=systems+engineer.

Tony Hayward was voted: Jacqui Goddard, "Embattled BP Chief: I Want My Life Back," *(London) Sunday Times*, May 31, 2010, available online to subscribers.

PAGE 182
When a boss goes off the rails: Figliuolo, discussion.

CHAPTER 13: RELATIONSHIP LESSONS

PAGE 188
Alan Beck, who researches: Beck, discussion.

PAGE 189
surveys by the American Pet Products Association: American Pet Products Association, "Industry Statistics & Trends," http://www.americanpetproducts.org/press_industrytrends.asp.

Studies also show that petting a dog: Kerstin Uvnäs-Moberg, "Role of Oxytocin in Human Animal Interaction," presented at "People & Animals: For Life," International Association of Human Animal Interaction Organisations, 12th annual international conference, July 1–4, 2010, plenary session 3, http://www.manimalis.se/uploads/4c3d5abbc74e04c3d5ab bc9041.pdf.

PAGES 189–190
In 2010...Americans spent $48.35 billion: "Industry Statistics & Trends," American Pet Products Association ("Spending: Total U.S. Pet Industry Expenditures"), http://www.americanpetproducts.org/press_industrytrends.asp.

PAGE 191

"I named him Need": Alan Beck and Aaron Katcher, *Between Pets and People: The Importance of Animal Companionship* (West Lafayette, IN: Purdue University Press, 1996) 45–46.

PAGE 192

Researchers have recently discovered that over one-third of these young offenders: Beck and Katcher, *Between Pets and People*, 48.

PAGE 193

As Beck noted in an interview, pets often serve: J. McNicholas and G. M. Collis, "Children's Representations of Pets in Their Social Networks," *Child: Care, Health Development*, vol. 27, no. 3 (May 2001): 279–94, http://onlinelibrary.wiley.com/doi/10.1046/j.1365-2214.2001.00202.x/abstract.

"There's growing evidence, too, that interaction with animals": Beck, discussion. Also see Anonymous, "Pets Foster Kids' Nurturing Skills," *Futurist* (January/February 1993): 8, http://pqasb.pqarchiver.com/futurist/access/1494391.html?FMT=ABS&FMTS=ABS:FT&type=current&date=Jan%2FFeb+1993&author=Anonymous&pub=The+Futurist&edition=&startpage=8&desc=Pets+foster+kids%27+nurturing+skills.

PAGE 194

Studies now show that children raised with pets: Dennis R. Ownby, MD, Christine Cole Johnson, MD, and Edward L. Peterson, PhD, "Exposure to Dogs and Cats in the First Year of Life and Risk of Allergic Sensitization at 6 to 7 Years of Age," *JAMA*, vol. 288, no. 8 (2002): 963–72, http://jama.ama-assn.org/content/288/8/963.full.

And they're also less likely to suffer from: Jane Heyworth, H. Cutt, and G. Glonek, "Does Dog or Cat Ownership Lead to Increased Gastroenteritis in Young Children in South Australia?" *Epidemiology and Infection*, vol. 134, no. 5 (2006): 926–34, http://journals.cambridge.org/abstract_S0950268806006078.

In a laboratory setting, students who spent time petting a dog: Karen Allen, Barbara E. Shykoff, and Joseph L. Izzo, Jr., " Pet Ownership, but Not ACE Inhibitor Therapy, Blunts Home Blood Pressure Responses to Mental Stress," *Hypertension*, vol. 38 (2001):815–20, http://hyper.ahajournals.org/cgi/content/full/38/4/815. Similar studies were reported by Diana Schellenberg, "A Friend Indeed," *Harvard Health Letter*, vol. 19, no. 2 (December 1993): 1–3.

A few years ago, Dr. Karen Allen: Karen M. Allen, Jim Blascovich, Joe Tomaka, and Robert M. Kelsey, "Presence of Human Friends and Pet Dogs as Moderators of Autonomic Responses to Stress in Women," *Journal of Personality and Social Psychology*, vol. 61, no. 4 (1991): 582–89, http://www.acsu.buffalo.edu/~kmallen/AllenPresence.pdf.

PAGE 196

Novelist Mary Gordon confessed: Mary Gordon, "The Empty Nest Dog," *More* (posted online January 27, 2010), http://www.more.com/relationships/attitudes/empty-nest-dog.

PAGE 197

In a blog for Psychology Today *magazine, Madora Kibbe*: Madora Kibbe "Women and the Dogs Who Walk Them," *Psychology Today* (blog, "My Empty Nest"), November 13, 2009, http://www.psychologytoday.com/blog/my-empty-nest/200911/women-and-the-dogs-who-walk-them.

PAGE 199

According to Dr. Edward Creagan: "PAWSitive Look at Pets and the Aging: Science Supports the Human-Animal Bond," PAWSitive InterAction, December 5, 2003, http://www.pawsitiveinteraction.com/pdf/WhitePaper-12_05_03.pdf. Also see "Pets and the Aging: Science Supports the Human-Animal Bond," PAWSitive InterAction, 2003, http://www.pawsitiveinteraction.com/pdf/White_paper-10_16_03.pdf.

Dr. Rebecca Johnson: "PAWSitive Look at Pets and the Aging: Science Supports the Human-Animal Bond," PAWSitive InterAction.

Patients with aggressive Alzheimer's: University of Nebraska Medical Center, "Research Shows Therapy Dogs Give Alzheimer's Patients Relief from Sundown Syndrome," press release, October 25, 1999, http://app1.unmc.edu/publicaffairs/newsarchive/view_art.cfm?article_id=931.

a study by researchers at the University of Kentucky: Thomas F. Garrity, Lorann Stallones, Martin B. Marx, and Timothy P. Johnson, "Pet Ownership and Attachment as Supportive Factors in the Health of the Elderly," *Anthrozoos*, vol. 3, no. 1 (1989): 35–44, www.deltasociety.org/?Document.Doc?id=317.

"A pet is a medication without side effects": Steve Dale, "Why Pets Are Good for Us," *USA Weekend*, July 25, 2010, http://www.usaweekend.com/article/20100723/HOME05/7250320/Why-pets-good-us.

PAGE 201

Dr. Karen Allen's research indicated: "Pet Ownership, but Not ACE Inhibitor Therapy, Blunts Home Blood Pressure Responses to Mental Stress," *Hypertension*.

Similarly, a team of researchers in Australia: W. P. Anderson, C. M. Reid, and G. L. Jennings, "Pet Ownership and Risk Factors for Cardiovascular Disease," *Medical Journal of Australia*, vol. 157, no. 5 (September 7, 1992): 298–301, http://www.ncbi.nlm.nih.gov/pubmed/1435469. Also see E. Friedmann and S. A. Thomas, "Pet Ownership, Social Support, and One-Year Survival After Acute Myocardial Infarction in the Cardiac Arrhythmia Suppression Trial (CAST)," *American Journal of Cardiology*, vol. 76, no. 17 (December 15, 1995): 1213–17.

CHAPTER 14: GENEROSITY AND GIVING BACK

PAGE 202

Raised in the Hotel Roosevelt: Samuel Ross (founder, Green Chimneys), in discussion with the author, September 2010.

PAGE 206

Consider Bruce FaBrizio: Bruce FaBrizio (founder, Sunshine Makers), in discussion with the author, October 2010.

PAGE 207

In Upstarts, *she profiles Bill Downing*: Donna Fenn, *Upstarts: How GenY Entrepreneurs are Rocking the Business World* (New York: McGraw Hill, 2010), 156–57.

PAGE 209

In fact, researchers in Australia found: Lisa J. Wood, Billie Giles-Corti, Max K. Bulsara, and Darcy A. Bosch, "More Than a Furry Companion: The Ripple Effect of Companion Animals on Neighborhood Interactions and Sense of Community," *Society & Animals*, vol. 15, no. 1 (October 30, 2008): 43–56, http://www.animalsandsociety.org/assets/library/638_morethanafurrycompanion.pdf.

First, I want to thank my pack at home. My wife, Brenda, who has believed in me throughout this entire project. Not only was she a constant inspiration, she contributed extensive research to this book. I also want to thank my sons, Rob and Josh, my mom, dad, and siblings, Cathy, Laura, and John, who believed I could do anything I set my mind to, sometimes in spite of myself.

Next, kudos to my dedicated and hardworking staff at the American Pet Products Association and The Impetus Agency for embracing the models of canine collaboration I have written about. And, of course, a thank-you to our special office dogs—Lola, Doyle, Perseus, Casey, and Bernie.

I'm also grateful to the American Pet Products Association for hiring me and allowing me to do a job I truly love.

My good friend Charles Miller served as my navigator through the many different stages of my management career. Dr. Marty Becker, the resident veterinarian on ABC's *Good Morning America,* encouraged me to tell my story, and truly believed in this book. And Allan Levey served as a role model for me, as well as for many others in the pet industry.

My good friends (you all know who you are) encouraged me throughout the writing process. A special thanks goes to Maureen and Tom Field, Paul Farris, and Deepak and Purnima Bramhavar.

I owe a good deal to the following experts who have explored the emotional IQ of dogs: Dr. Alan Beck of Purdue University; Susan Tripp, founder of the Animal Behavior Network; Patricia Olsen, former head of the Morris Animal League; and Dr. Samuel Ross, the founder of Green Chimneys, a truly miraculous place where animals lead troubled kids to a better place in life. Inspired by their work, APPA has supported the Human Animal Bond Research Initiative (HABRI).

I'm grateful to Debra Tosch, Executive Director of the Search Dog Foundation, and agility expert Julia Wolfe of Acton, California, for their stories about training high-performing dogs, and to all the business leaders who graciously consented to be interviewed for this book: Elizabeth Kirkhart, PhD, cofounder of Moving Boundaries; Carol Kallendorf, at Delta Associates; Matt Broder at Pitney Bowes; Kathy Clinton at Autodesk; Carol Chapin and Denise Dochnahl at Simple Green; Jeanine Falcon at Replacements Ltd; Robin Koval at the Kaplan-Thaler Group; Dr. Zeev Neuwirth at Harvard Vanguard Health; Bill Scudder at Sonusnet; consultants Stanton Smith, Steve Arneson, and Mike Figliuolo; Margaret Callaway of Callaway Associates; Fred Seddiqui of Silicon Valley Venture Partners; and Generation Y expert Donna Fenn.

I have been fortunate indeed in my publisher, Glenn Yeffeth, the founder of BenBella Books, and appreciate the nurturing of his marketing director, Adrienne Lang, as well as the support and good humor of my agent, Harvey Klinger.

Another special thank-you to my coauthor, Valerie Andrews, aka the Media Muse, whose hard work and dogged determination helped bring this book to life.

Last, I want to acknowledge the dogs who have served as my inspirations: my first dog, Duke, followed by Lady and Jigg; my college fraternity's cadre of Saint Bernards; Shannon, the Irish setter who joined me as I began my working career; and my three golden retrievers—Samson, who taught me the benefit of wandering beyond the usual boundaries; Wharf, who showed me the importance of gentleness, loyalty, and forgiveness; and Dakota, who gave me lessons in creativity, patience, and good humor.

Dogs make sure we have a reason to get up in the morning, they make us feel needed, and they just plain make us feel good. And so to these wonderful creatures, I say thank you for bringing me so much happiness and for teaching me so much.

ROBERT VETERE is president of the American Pet Products Association, the world's largest trade organization for pet products.

Over the past two decades, he has led management training seminars using the insights in this book. Among the Fortune 500 companies he has counseled are Union Carbide, First Brands, Wal-Mart, Clorox, Lehman Brothers, Merck, Oil-Dri, Mars, Nestlé, Bear Stearns, PetSmart, Church & Dwight, IDEXX Laboratories, Hartz Mountain Industries, and Procter & Gamble, as well the Gerson Lehrman Group, a technology consulting company that serves 129 firms on the Fortune list.

He has been interviewed by *Businessweek*, *The Wall Street Journal*, *Kiplinger's Personal Finance Magazine*, *Entrepreneur* magazine, *ABC-TV Early Show* and *World News Tonight*, CBS News, CNN, *The New York Times* magazine, *The Washington Post*, *USA Today*, and the *Chicago Tribune*. The public relations firm The Impetus Agency routinely schedules his speaking engagements, securing well over 200 major television and radio appearances and print interviews a year. He also writes a popular blog on the pet industry introducing high-end products by Ralph

Lauren and Gianni Versace as well as novelty items like lizard jewelry and ferret hammocks.

At APPA, Bob works with Dr. Marty Becker of ABC's *Good Morning America* and Dr. Alan Beck at Purdue University to explore the human-animal bond. He also volunteers at Green Chimneys, a farm that teaches leadership skills to children with emotional, social, and learning disabilities.

Before joining APPA, Bob served as senior vice president, administration, general counsel, and secretary at Oil-Dri Corporation of America, a publicly traded $175 million international manufacturer of agricultural, industrial, and pet products. His management responsibilities encompassed human resources, environmental health and safety, product compliance, and government relations. His achievements at Oil-Dri range from restructuring the law and human resources departments to successfully negotiating a new labor contract with the United Steelworkers Union. Bob also spent twenty-five years at First Brands Corporation, makers of GLAD Wrap and Bags, Prestone Antifreeze, and Jonny Cat Litter, serving as general counsel/director of government relations, senior corporate counsel, senior corporate staff engineer, and corporate director of professional development.

As a journalist, **VALERIE ANDREWS** has spent over 25 years chronicling social innovation. Her work has appeared in major magazines, on PBS television, and the web. She recently coauthored *The Business of Changing Lives: How One Company Took the Information Superhighway to the Inner City* with Allan Weis, one of the founders of the Internet, and has edited several bestselling authors. Her articles about creativity, peak performance, and changes in the American workplace have appeared in *People*, *New York*, *Vogue*, and *Esquire*. She has also appeared as a commentator on Public Television and is the author of *A Passion for This Earth*, essays on our connection to the natural world. Her first book, *The Psychic Power of Running*, was published by Rawson Associates.

Bibliography

BOOKS ABOUT CANINE INTELLIGENCE

Beck, Alan. *The Ecology of Stray Dogs: A Study of Free-Ranging Urban Animals.* West Lafayette, IN: Purdue University Press, 2002.

Beck, Alan, and Aaron Katcher. *Between Pets and People: The Importance of Animal Companionship.* West Lafayette, IN: Purdue University Press, 1996.

Becker, Marty, and Gina Spadafori. *Your Dog: The Owner's Manual: Hundreds of Secrets, Surprises, and Solutions for Raising a Happy, Healthy Dog.* New York: Grand Central Life & Style, 2011.

Coppinger, Raymond, and Lorna Coppinger. *Dogs: A Startling New Understanding of Canine Origin, Behavior and Evolution.* Chicago: University of Chicago Press, 2002.

Coren, Stanley. *How Dogs Think: What the World Looks Like to Them and Why They Act the Way They Do.* New York: Free Press, 2005.

———. *The Intelligence of Dogs: A Guide to the Thoughts, Emotions, and Inner Lives of Our Canine Companions.* New York: Free Press, 2005.

Daley Olmert, Meg. *Made for Each Other: The Biology of the Human-Animal Bond.* Philadelphia: Da Capo Press, 2009.

Grandin, Temple, and Catherine Johnson. *Animals Make Us Human: Creating the Best Life for Animals*. Boston: Mariner Books, 2010.

Hannah, Barbara. *The Cat, Dog, and Horse Lectures, and "The Beyond."* Edited by Dean L. Frantz. Wilmette, IL: Chiron Publications, 2004.

Hearne, Vicki. *Adam's Task: Calling Animals by Name*. New York: Skyhorse Publishing, 2007.

Markoe, Merrill. *What the Dogs Have Taught Me: And Other Amazing Things I've Learned*. New York: Villard, 2005.

Marshall Thomas, Elizabeth. *The Hidden Life of Dogs*. New York: Mariner Books, 2010.

——. *The Social Lives of Dogs: The Grace of Canine Company*. New York: PocketBooks, 2000.

Morris, Desmond. *Dogwatching: Why Dogs Bark and Everything Else You Ever Wanted to Know*. New York: Three Rivers Press, 1986.

Moussaieff Masson, Jeffrey. *Dogs Never Lie About Love: Reflections on the Emotional World of Dogs*. New York: Three Rivers Press, 1998.

Palika, Liz, and Jennifer Fearing. *Dogs at Work: A Practical Guide to Creating Dog-Friendly Workplaces*. Washington, DC: Humane Society Press, 2008.

Ross, Samuel B., Jr. *The Extraordinary Spirit of Green Chimneys: Connecting Children and Animals to Create Hope*. West Lafayette, IN: Purdue University Press, 2011.

Serpell, James. *In the Company of Animals: A Study of Human-Animal Relationships*. Cambridge: Cambridge University Press, 1996.

Shepard, Paul. *Thinking Animals: Animals and the Development of Human Intelligence*. Athens: University of Georgia Press, 1998.

Telesco, Patricia. *Dog Spirit: Hounds, Howlings, and Hocus-Pocus*. Rochester, VT: Destiny Books, 2000.

Vilmos, Csányi. *If Dogs Could Talk: Exploring the Canine Mind*. New York: North Point Press, 2005.

Woloy, Eleanora M. *The Symbol of the Dog in the Human Psyche: A Study of the Human-Dog Bond*. Wilmette, IL: Chiron Publications, 1990.

GREAT DOG STORIES

Shinto, Jeanne, ed. *The Literary Dog: Great Contemporary Dog Stories*. New York: Atlantic Monthly Press, 1990.

Wroblewski, David. *The Story of Edgar Sawtelle*. New York: Ecco, 2008.

BOOKS ABOUT DOGGED MANAGEMENT

Arneson, Steve. *Bootstrap Leadership: 50 Ways to Break Out, Take Charge, and Move Up*. San Francisco: Berrett-Koehler Publishers, 2010.

Baldoni, John. *Lead by Example: 50 Ways Great Leaders Inspire Results*. New York: AMACOM, 2009.

Belding, Shaun. *Winning with the Employee from Hell: A Guide to Performance and Motivation*. Toronto: ECW Press, 2004.

Cockerell, Lee. *Creating Magic: 10 Common Sense Leadership Strategies from a Life at Disney*. New York: Doubleday, 2008.

Dotlich, David L., and Peter C. Cairo. *Why CEOs Fail: The 11 Behaviors That Can Derail Your Climb to the Top and How to Manage Them*. San Francisco: Jossey-Bass, 2003.

Fenn, Donna. *Upstarts! How GenY Entrepreneurs Are Rocking the World of Business and 8 Ways You Can Profit from Their Success*. New York: McGraw Hill, 2010.

Hsieh, Tony. *Delivering Happiness: A Path to Profits, Passion, and Purpose*. New York: Business Plus, 2010.

Jacobs, Charles S. *Management Rewired: Why Feedback Doesn't Work and Other Surprising Lessons from the Latest Brain Science*. New York: Portfolio, 2010.

Kaplan Thaler, Linda, and Robin Koval. *The Power of Nice: How to Conquer the Business World with Kindness*. New York: Crown Business, 2006.

———. *The Power of Small: Why Little Things Make All the Difference*. New York: Crown Business, 2009.

Kinsey Goman, Carol. *The Nonverbal Advantage: Secrets and Science of Body Language at Work*. San Francisco: Berrett-Koehler Publishers, 2008.

Sutton, Robert I. *Good Boss, Bad Boss: How to Be the Best ... and Learn from the Worst*. New York: Business Plus, 2010.

Thomas, Kenneth W. *Intrinsic Motivation at Work: What Really Drives Employee Engagement*. 2nd edition. San Francisco: Berrett-Koehler Publishers, 2009.

**Center for the Human-Animal Bond at Purdue University
School of Veterinary Medicine**

www.vet.purdue.edu/chab/

Human-Animal Bond Research Initiative

http://www.habri.org/about.html

Search Dog Foundation

www.searchdogfoundation.org

Take Your Dog to Work Day

http://www.takeyourdog.com/

The Animal Behavior Network

www.animalbehavior.net/

American Pet Products Association

www.americanpetproducts.org